Dear Graham,
... Kierkegaard,
... this
... this

Remains of the Raj

The British Legacy in India

ANTONY WILD

REMAINS OF THE RAJ

The British Legacy in India

HarperCollins*Publishers*

First published in 2001 by HarperCollins*Publishers*
77–85 Fulham Palace Road
London W6 8JB

The HarperCollins website address is
www.fireandwater.com

A CIP catalogue record for this book is available from the British Library.

ISBN: 0 00 711428 1

Design: Caroline Hill
Index: Sue Martin
Cartography: Cosmographics, Watford

06 05 04 03 02 01
8 7 6 5 4 3 2 1

Colour reproduction by Colourscan Pte. Ltd
Printed and bound in Singapore by Imago

PAGE 2 **The narrow-gauge train from Kalka to Simla. The mighty rulers of the Raj followed in her tracks.**

Picture credits

Pages 1, 52–53, 97, 209, 213 © Hutchison Picture Library,
63, 67, 151, 153, 197(l), 221 © Horner/Hutchison Picture Library,
64 © Taylor/Hutchison Picture Library, 72 © Singer/Hutchison Picture Library,
76, 192–193 © Francis/Hutchison Picture Library (t), 109 © Brinicombe/Hutchison Picture Library, 126(b) © Freire/Hutchison Picture Library, 128–129, 167(r) © Hart/Hutchison Picture Library, 143 © Highet/Hutchison Picture Library, 181© Page/Hutchison Picture Library, 190, 116, 206 © Pemberton/Hutchison Picture Library
Pages 2, 75, 124 © Chris Caldicott
Pages 7, 8, 9, 14, 31, 44 76(b), 78, 91, 118, 126(t), 132, 133, 134, 135, 152, 154, 167(l), 176, 178, 183, 184, 185, 186, 187, 198, 199, 216, 224, 230, 235 © Charlotte Cory
Page 12(t) © from C. R Markham, *Memoir of the India Survey* (c.1870)
page 12 (b) © By courtesy of the Survey of India
Pages 16, 92, 182, 219 © By courtesy of the National Portrait Gallery
Pages 17, 21, 35, 36, 37, 39, 43, 47, 149, 195 © Getty Images Ltd
Pages 18 © National Maritime Museum
Pages 20, 24–25, 40, 50, 74, 81, 127, 131, 144, 160, 189, 197(r), 201, 220 © Antonio Martinelli
Pages 22, 56, 57, 69 © V & A Picture Library
Page 27 © Tate Gallery, London
Pages 28, 71 © Art Achive
Page 32 © British Library
Pages 48–49, 215 © Robert Harding Picture Library
Pages 55 © Rai/Magnum Photos, 158–159, 194 © Magnum Photos, 226, 227 © Parr/Magnum Photos
Pages 59, 138 © Christie's Images
Pages 77 © Images of India, 111, 115 © Orde Eliason/Link, 119 © Anil Dave/Images of India, 203 © Cooper/Images of India, 231 © Bigland/Images of India
Pages 82, 85, 86, 87, 98, 104, 106 © Courtesy of the Director, National Army Museum, London
Page 89 © Reuters/Popperfoto
Pages 93, 101, 120 © Ann & Bury Peerless
Pages 94–95 © Vieti Collection/Trip, 103 © Trip, 121 © Lal/Trip, 123, 162 © Rogers/Trip, 125, 218 © Dinodia/Trip, 136 © Lester/Trip, 137 © Tovy/Trip, 148 © Good/Trip, 161 © Burrows/Trip, 210 © Bognar/Trip.
Pages 100, 140, 141, 169 © Richard House
Page 113 © Imperial War Museum
Page 114 © Pamela Singh
Page 147 © Kevin Rushby
Pages 156, 164 (b), 171, 217, 222 © Thomas Kelly
Pages 157, 173 © Royal Geographical Society, London
Page 164(t) © Bernard Woods
Pages 174 © Julia Keay
Page 175 © Kirsty Chakravarty, Courtesy of the Survey of India
Pages 228, 229 © Vinod Dua
Page 233 © MGM (Courtesy Kobal)
Page 225 © HarperCollins*Publishers*

With special thanks to the Assam Company Ltd for providing pictures on pages 60 and 61.

Charlotte Cory is a novelist, travel writer and photographer. She has published three novels, *The Unforgiving, The Laughter of Fools* and *The Guest* and is currently writing a fantastical book based on a diary written in Victorian Ceylon (Sri Lanka) by an Anglo-Irish girl. Entitled *Imperial Quadrille*, this story of Empire, time and memory will be published in Spring 2003 by HarperCollins. Charlotte travelled to India courtesy of Western & Oriental, a travel company that specialises in the Indian subcontinent. She writes regularly for the *The Daily Telegraph*.

CONTENTS

LEFT 'Many ladies keep no *ayah*; the implements one requires are few, and consist chiefly of dusters, brushes & c. The *ayah's* duties naturally vary immensely with her situation. If there are no children, she is virtually a lady's maid, while if an English nurse is kept, her responsibilities are almost *nil*. On the other hand, when she is really head nurse, she is of all the servants the most important'. *The Complete Indian Housekeeper and Cook*, published, 1898.

DEFINITIONS, APOLOGIES, ACKNOWLEDGEMENTS

The East India Company was officially chartered by Queen Elizabeth I in 1600, as 'The Governor and Company of Merchants of London trading into the East Indies'. In 1709, it merged with another company trading to the East to form 'the United Company of Merchants of England trading to the East Indies'. As a result of the Charter Act of 1833 the Company was afterwards officially referred to as 'The East India Company'. The India Act of 1858 saw the end of the Company as an active entity, but the winding-up process was not finally accomplished until 1874, when its last Charter expired. The East Indies were defined by the 1600 Charter as anything east of the Cape of Good Hope, which came at one stage to include Vancouver in Western Canada. Coincidentally Bengal, scene of the Company's first great territorial success, was in what became known geographically as East India.

As this book includes the period before Partition in 1947, the terms 'Indian' or 'India' should be taken as meaning the people or lands of the subcontinent, including Pakistan and Bangladesh.
The term 'servants' in connection with the Company, means any of its employees, from the Governor-General to the lowliest clerk. Elsewhere, the term is used conventionally.

After 1858, India was run directly by the Crown, a Viceroy was appointed, and Victoria became the Empress of India in 1876. The term 'raj' has come to be associated with British Crown rule in India between 1858 and Independence in 1947; here it is used in the general sense, derived from Sanskrit meaning 'rule'. Hence, the 'Company's raj' refers to the period of the Company's domination of most or major parts of India until 1858. This book's title, *Remains of the Raj,* covers the remains from the period of British rule in India, whether by Company or Crown.

In India, and in the more politically sensitive of occidental histories, the disturbance in India in 1857 is frequently called the first war of independence. Here, with due apologies, it is termed 'the Mutiny'.

The term 'the English' includes, again with apologies, the Scots, the Irish and the Welsh during the Company era; I use the term 'the English' during the Company era and 'the British' during the period when India was ruled by the Crown, as distinct from the Company. This is merely a convenient way of distinguishing the rulers during the two consecutive Raj.

The history of the British Raj is the subject of enduring fascination for academics, amateur historians and laymen alike, and there is no shortage of meticulously researched books on virtually any aspect of the Raj that one might care to imagine. For most of the material in this volume I am deeply indebted to such specialist researches, and the writings of others. Space prohibits mentioning them all, but if any one in particular could be described as the foundation on which this book rests it would, appropriately enough, be Jan Morris' *Stones of Empire.*

Present-day India and Pakistan are now the stars of the subcontinent's triumvirate, and the paucity of material relating to Bangladesh in this book reflects the relative oblivion to which the former 'Golden Bengal' has been consigned. Practically unphotographed and unsung (with the exception of George Harrison's eponymous album) Bangladesh today is the poorest of poor relations, with the stark prospect of rising sea levels compounding its already overwhelming problems.

Thanks are also due to my agent, Gillon Aitken; Polly Powell at HarperCollins who championed this work; and to Victoria Alers-Hankey, who edited it, as well as undertaking the onerous task of finding the pictures corresponding to my whims; and Charlotte Cory, whose help with the captions for the many photographs she provided was much appreciated; the family de Gunzburg were providers of intellectual, spiritual and temporal nourishment, and the forbearing Hector and Girl nobly sacrificed many of their walks for the greater good of this work. I hope I have served them all well.

Normandy, May 2001.

LEFT The cast iron drain cover from outside the Viceregal Lodge, Simla.

PREFACE

'Surprises crackle, like electric arcs between the interfaces of culture. These interfaces are where history now seeks itself; they will be the historical sites of the future.'

Robert Hughes *The Culture of Complaint*

It is a common experience for a first-time traveller from the British Isles to be struck by the Britishness of India. In scale, this ranges from the use of language on the tickets for trains, to the 'Indo-Saracenic' grandeur of the Victorian railway terminii from which they issue forth. Typically, this apparent Britishness has a preserved-in-aspic quality, as if time's passage had ground to a halt at Independence in 1947 and the consequence had been gathering dust ever since. This has resulted in a 'look-how-quaint-it-is' view of the British legacy in India which both underestimates the staggering size and pervasiveness of that legacy, as well as running the risk of being grossly patronising to the Indians themselves, as if they were mere custodians of some sort of Raj theme park. The much-touted western view that Indians themselves are nostalgic about the British times is probably less the result because of an inherent love for the British themselves than for the order and lack of corruption that came with them. Had the Raj been as smoothly run by Russians, Indians might well feel the same towards them now. The archetypal old Etonian nawab speaking an English straight out of a Noel Coward play understandably distracts the visitor's attention from the monumental ubiquity of the remains of the Raj: if one could still find in the English countryside native aristocrats who dressed in togas and spoke perfect Emperor's Latin, we would likewise probably find them more diverting than the technical feat that is Watling Street. Because it is more recent in its passing, the inheritance of Britain's Indian Empire has not yet acquired all the lineaments of pukka history.

One result of this is that the trivial and the important are still mixed up in the historical soup that was the Raj. Over time they will undoubtedly separate, and the unimportant things will rise to the surface and be thrown aside, and the serious business of history will take precedence – analysis of wars, treaties, grand architecture, leaders, the law. In the meantime we are in the privileged position of being able to witness an Empire shortly after the fall. It is only fifty years or so since the last English officers' cries echoed across a dusty parade ground; the last white District Commissioner presided over a native durbar, or the last memsahib sweltered in the first-class waiting room. In India, at times it seems as if all that would be required would be a very modest time-machine for their ghosts to corporealise again, such is the sense of the proximity of the British presence there. However, *Remains of the Raj* sets out to examine not just the colonists' footprints in the Indian dust, but the way in which shards of Britishness have become part of a living tradition.

RIGHT The most famous view in the world was nearly destroyed by one Governor-General, Lord Bentinck, who only baulked at the idea of shifting the derelict Taj Mahal back to England in pieces when he learnt of the likely cost. A later Viceroy, Lord Curzon, initiated the preservation work and the addition of the English lawns (above) which saved it for posterity.

THE INDIAN SUBCONTINENT
see insert for detail
Bokhara
Herat
Bamian
Kabul
N.W.F.P.
Jalalabad
KASHMIR
Maiwand
Ghazni
Khyber Pass
Attock
Rawalpindi
Peshawar
Khandahar
PUNJAB
Lahore
Firozpur
Simla
LADAKH
TIBET
Lhasa
BALUCHISTAN
Quetta
Bolan Pass
R. Indus
Meerut
Delhi
Ranikhet
Nainital
NEPAL
Himalayas
Mt. Everest
BHUTAN
SIKKIM
Darjeeling
R. Brahmaputra
SIND
Mohenjo Daro
PAKISTAN
Jaipur
Agra
R. Ganges
Etawah
Lucknow
R. Gumpti
Cawnpore
OUDH
Benares
Patna
BENGAL
ASSAM
Haflong
Karachi
RAJASTHAN
R. Chambal
Gwalior
Allahabad
Chunar
R. Ganges
BANGLADESH
Sanchi
Jhansi
BIHAR
Plassey
Barrrackpore
Bhopal
R. Narmada
Sironj
Calcutta
Port Hooghli
R. Hooghli
GUJERAT
Ahmadabad
Dabhoi
Dandi
Surat
Swalley Hole
R. Mahanadi
Cox's Bazar
Nagpur
Hinganghat
MAHARASHTRA
WESTERN GHATS
Eastern Ghats
Bombay
Poona
R. Godavari
ANDHRA PRADESH
ARABIAN SEA
Sevedroog
Konkan Coast
BAY OF BENGAL
Geriah
Secunderabad
Hyderabad
R. Krishna
CARNATIC
DECCAN
Goa
Mangalore
Bangalore
Madras
Seringapatam
Mysore
Pondicherry
Malabar Coast
Calicut
Ootacamund
Coimbatore
R. Cavvery
Tanjore
Cochin
TRAVANCORE
Madurai
Rameshwaram
Thiruvananthapuram
Cape Comorin
CEYLON
INDIAN OCEAN
Kashgar
Bozai Gumbaz
WAKHAN
Chitral
Dartok
Hunza
Gilgit
Mustagh Pass
Leh
LADAKH
Jalalabad
Khyber Pass
Hoti Mardan
Murree
Srinigar
Attock
Nowshera
Peshawar
R. Indus
Rawalpindi
KASHMIR
Lahore
Dharamsala
Corbett Nat.Pk.
Mussoorie
Amritsar
Firozpur
Simla
Solan
Dehra Dun
Meerut
Delhi
R. Sutlej
THE NORTH WEST FRONTIER

THE SUBCONTINENT SHOWING PAGE NUMBERS OF ILLUSTRATIONS

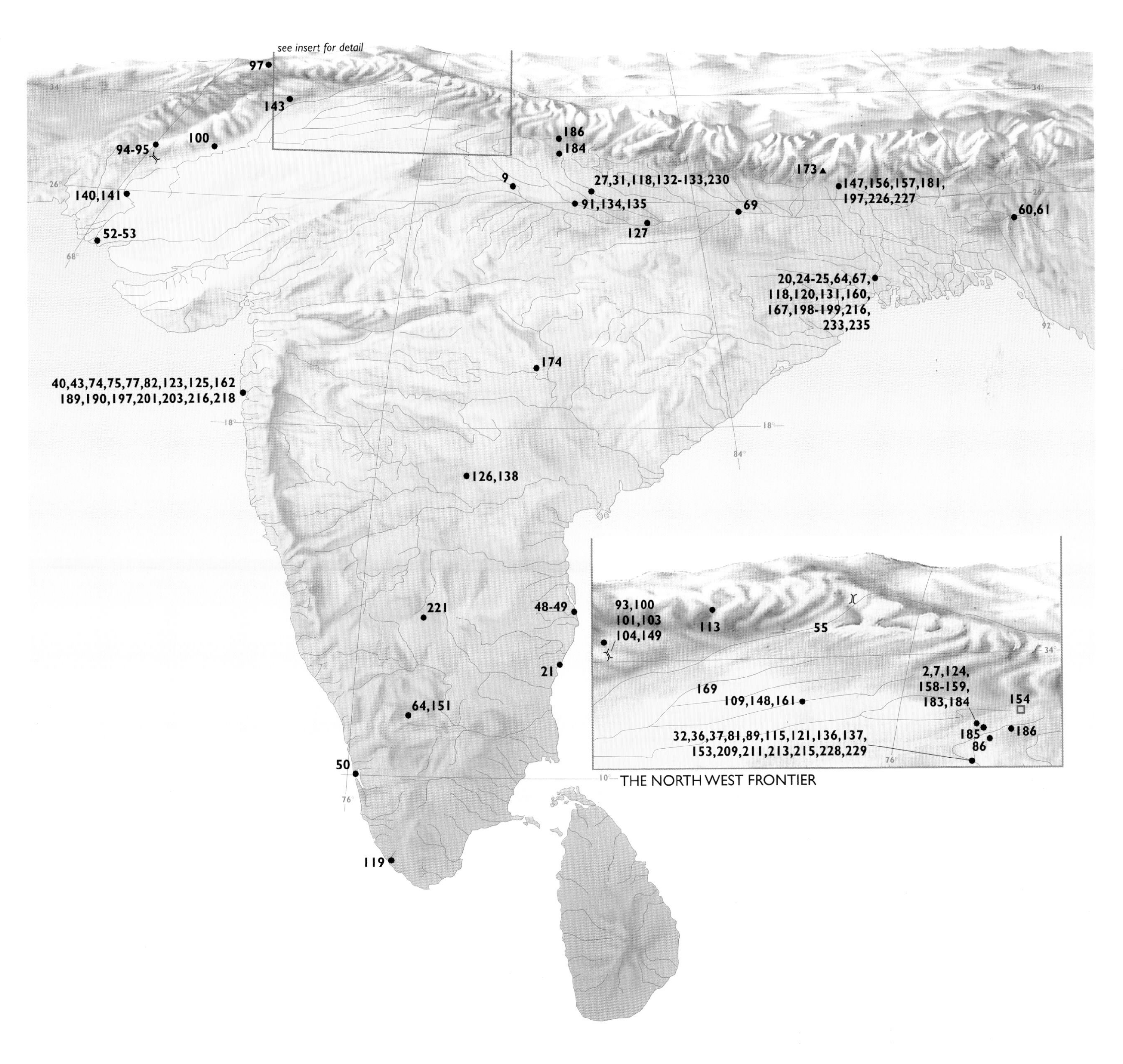

RIGHT The Great Trigonometrical Survey at its completion in 1870. The north-south axis was originated by William Lambton and completed by George Everest. Map making was an essential precursor to the great civil engineering projects initiated in India by the British in the second half of the nineteenth century.

RIGHT The tower of the magnificent eleventh-century temple at Tangore in south India. The map makers of Empire used a vantage point whether natural or man-made. The Great Theodolite (see page 175) was winched to the top of this tower – a delicate operation during which the Theodolite slipped and smashed into the carved statuary.

BRITISH INDIA, 1931

I

HISTORICAL PERSPECTIVE

Detail of the gate
leading to the Cawnpore
Memorial, the sanctum
sanctorum of the Raj.

From trade to territory

The intentions of the 218 knights and merchants of the City of London who formed the East India Company, and those of Queen Elizabeth I who granted its Royal Charter on 31 December 1600, were barely matched by the outcome. The venture failed to achieve its stated objectives – it made little impression on the Dutch control of the spice trade and could not establish a lasting outpost in the East Indies in the early years. Yet it succeeded beyond all measure in establishing military dominance and a political empire for Britain in India. The innumerable Indian wars, the shattering Mutiny, the pomp and display of the Delhi Durbar and the tragedy of Partition were all initiated by Elizabeth's characteristically flamboyant signature on a charter designed simply to provide a monopoly on trading rights to the east of the Cape of Good Hope for a limited period of fifteen years to a consortium of city businessmen. The tension between the straightforward commercial aims of the Company's Court of Directors in London, who simply desired that it should be able to trade profitably and peacefully, and the opportunist vision of its servants sent to implement its policies, continued well into the nineteenth century. Even Robert Clive's astonishing military achievements met with a chorus of disapproval from his superiors at home. Time and geographical distance made the attempts of the Directors to direct impossible, and ultimately it lay in the hands of its officers to make what they could of the prevailing situation in the field. This was done with such a vengeance and so successfully that by 1834, whilst nominally still a company with shareholders and Directors in the ordinary way, the East India Company had ceased to be trade at all, and was instead authorised ruler of the vast Indian subcontinent and numerous other possessions. The 'Jewel in the Crown', later to be cherished by Queen-Empress Victoria, was in effect the Company's most valuable contract.

Above Queen Elizabeth I of England tramples upon Europe. She realised the importance of trade, and her signature on the East India Company Charter of 1600 gave rise to the Empire in the East.

Opposite Queen Victoria, Empress of India, not remotely amused. The official coronation portrait from 1877 shows her suitably installed on a splendid ivory throne by the Rajah of Travancore.

To understand how this transformation from trade to territory took place it is important to look into the changing role of Britain on the international stage. The history of the East India Company and that of its native country are in this respect inseparable. Up until the late Elizabethan age England was regarded by the then dominant European powers of Spain and France as an uncultured, barbarian nation snapping at the heels of its more civilised neighbours. Spain had seized enormous wealth for itself, largely in the form of bullion, from its colonies in South and Central America, and by forcibly taking Portugal under its wing in 1580, it was adding to its portfolio that country's formidable eastern trading empire. The Portuguese had developed the lucrative spice trade, first from India and later from the source of the most valuable spices themselves, the mysterious Spice Islands, now known as the Moluccas. However, the temporarily united Spain and Portugal was weaker than its components, and their war in the Netherlands had not only strained its resources but led, in

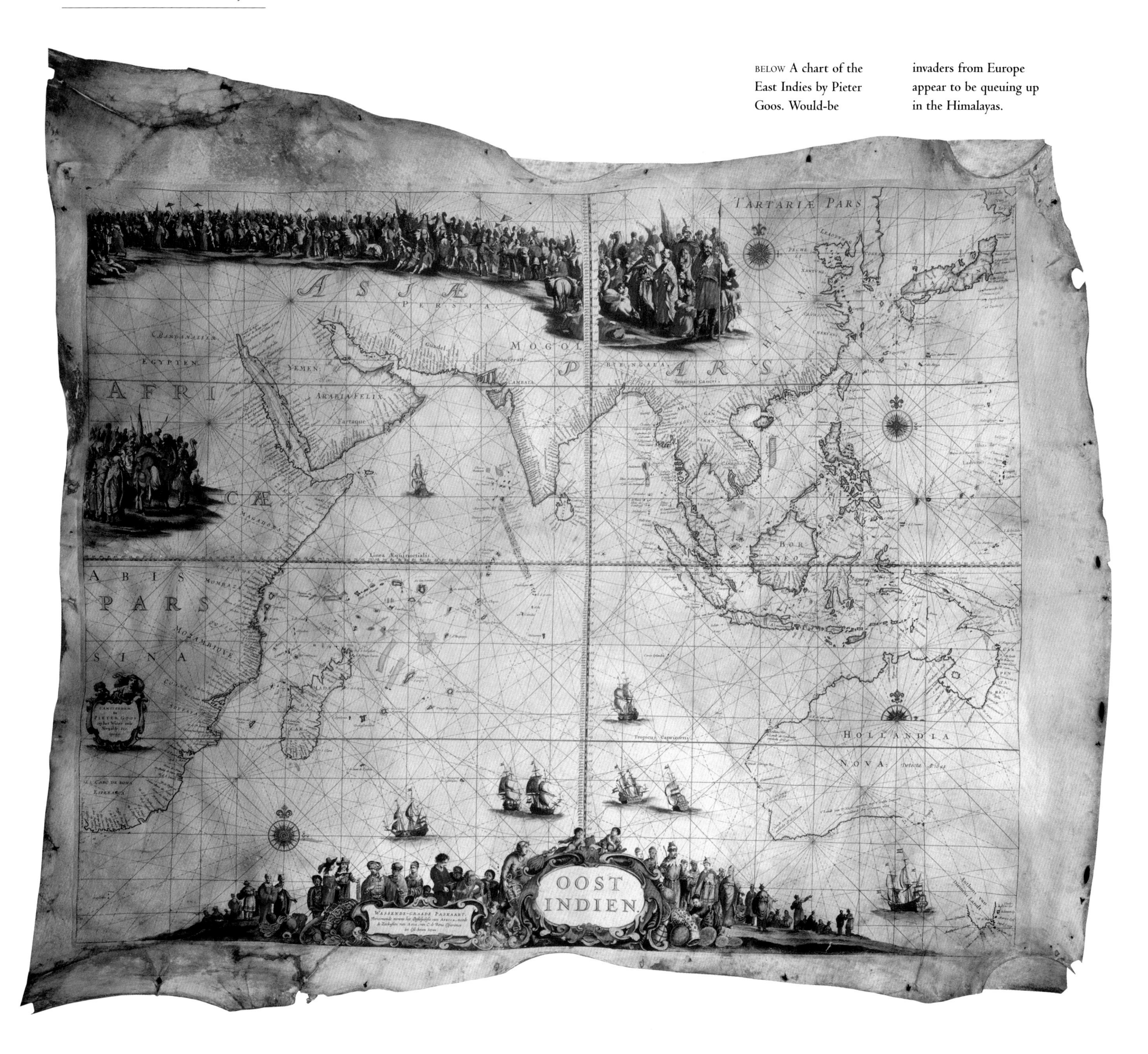

BELOW A chart of the East Indies by Pieter Goos. Would-be invaders from Europe appear to be queuing up in the Himalayas.

1579, to the creation of the United Provinces, later Holland. It was the newly-independent Dutch who would be resourceful enough to fill the vacuum left by the Portuguese in the East, and to gain control of the spice trade.

In the meantime, the activities of Sir Francis Drake, for all the vaunted status of his defeat of the Spanish Armada, were in reality those of a licensed pirate, and unlike the Dutch, the English lacked a coordinated maritime trading strategy. However, City merchants were well aware of the potential of foreign trading ventures, particularly after the death of Philip II in 1598 had further loosened Spain's global grip. They had promoted the nascent capitalist culture which had led to the foundation of the Mucovy, Levant and Virginia Companies, and now turned their attention to the East Indies. The publication in 1595 of charts stolen by Jan van Linschoten from the Archbishop of Goa had confirmed the exact location of the Spice Islands, and the East India Company was formed, financed and formally chartered; the 'First Voyage' of four ships set sail for the Spice Islands in 1601.

Much to his chagrin, Captain James Lancaster, its experienced commander, discovered that he was too late; the Dutch had unfortunately established themselves there first, and the Company was reduced to picking up scraps of trade, either by piracy or dealing through intermediaries, which became a reasonably profitable business. Perhaps this semi-piratical role appealed to some wild, improvisational streak deep in the national psyche; as when the Company needed to supplement its revenues, they realised that by getting involved in the existing local trade networks of the Indian Ocean they could exchange Indian cloths for spices in Batavia, their base near modern-day Jakarta. Thus, they started to explore the India coastline, and to encroach upon existing trade links between India, Java, Sumatra and the Middle East.

The successive embassies to the Moghul Court of Captain William Hawkins, whose hard drinking appealed so much to the alcoholic Emperor Jehangir that he made him commander of his cavalry, and the courtly demeanour of Sir Thomas Roe which made him a worthy rival to the polished Portuguese then influential at court, won the Company trading concessions at the port of Surat. The Emperor was particularly impressed by the Company's victory in a naval battle with the Portuguese at Swalley Hole, off Surat, in 1613. Control of the seas, especially the vital pilgrims' route along the Persian coast to Mecca, was not a matter to be trifled with, and if the English might prove to be more powerful than the Portuguese, their favour needed to be curried. Jehangir's modest concessions ultimately proved fatal to his Empire and within less than two hundred years most of it would be in the hands of the Company, the last of the Moghuls exiled to Burma.

ABOVE The Writers' Building, Calcutta, by Thomas and William Daniell, 1788. Built to house the lowly clerks employed to keep track of the Company's windfall of the Bengal tax revenues. The memorial to the dead of the so-called 'Black Hole', erected on the basis of an extremely dubious eye-witness account, was quietly moved elsewhere shortly after.

Meanwhile, the Spice Islands had yielded nutmeg of consolation, and the one tiny island in the Banda group held by the Company in the King's name became a source of such pride to James I that he styled himself 'King of England, Scotland, Ireland, France . . . and Pulo Run'. Attempting further to increase their presence in the Spice Islands inevitably brought clashes with the well-armed and well-financed Dutch East India Company. The massacre of Company factors by the perfidious Hollanders at Amboyna in 1623 put paid to such vain ambitions. However, Pulo Run was later exchanged for Manhattan, a real estate transaction that might still cause the Dutch an occasional twinge of regret. The Company retreated to settlements on the south-west coast of Sumatra, where it established pepper groves using indentured labour, an early example of the plantation system which was further developed when tea was introduced to India.

By the middle of the seventeenth century the East India Company could be found trading alongside Arab and Indian merchants in the East, and the Company was shipping goods as diverse as cloth from southern India to Sumatra, and coffee from Arabia to India. The profits thus generated were ploughed back into buying the spices required at home, and so they found a rather tortuous means of circumventing the Dutch stranglehold on that trade. It also meant they started to appreciate the vast wealth and trading potential of India itself. Gradually, they built up their power base, opening up a number of trading posts: Madras in 1639, Bombay in 1668 and Calcutta in 1690. These ports became known as the Presidencies, and were provided with all the necessaries for secure and prosperous trading – a Governor, a fort, a church (complete with a graveyard), warehouses, and later clubs, residential suburbs and pleasure gardens. Around the English enclaves sprang up native towns to house those who facilitated trading activities or in other ways made life easier – servants, palanquin bearers, moneylenders, banians (agents) and bibis (mistresses). The Presidencies were effectively built up from scratch by the Company, and they remain the principal cities of India today.

The English did not have it all their own way in India; other European nations were vying for trading privileges, such as the Portuguese who had long been established in their stronghold of Goa from which they were finally dislodged only in 1961. However, their influence was on the wane, especially after the destruction by the Moghuls of their trading post at Port Hoogli, Bengal in 1632.

At various times during the next two hundred years the Company had to compete with its equivalents from Holland, Denmark, the Holy Roman Empire, Sweden, and, most significantly, France. During the mid-eighteenth century, France had made great efforts to emulate the Company's success. Had it not been for some good luck allied to good leadership in the field from Clive and Eyre Coote, the French might well have managed to eject the English from southern India entirely. As it happened, the English learnt a great deal about how to turn Indian political instability to their advantage; to counter the machinations of the French Governor Dupleix down the coast from Madras at Pondicherry, they had to develop local alliances and make small-scale territorial forays.

LEFT **Old rivals, new playing field. The East India Company against Compagnie des Indes at Pondicherry circa 1788. For some years the outcome was in the balance and the Raj might easily have been French.**

HONI SOIT QVI MAL Y PENSE
DIEV ET MON DROIT

Thus the Company soon found itself in a new role as 'king maker', being able to make or break the ambitions of many a contender for a local throne. The fragmented nature of the subcontinent's political structure and the violent, turbulent divisions within local kingdoms played into the Company's hands. European trade, European weapons and European military training were pivotal in furthering the ambitions of any hopeful ruler who, once installed, would remain duly grateful and mostly compliant. Nowhere was this policy pursued with more success than in Bengal where, under Clive's command, the Company installed a succession of rulers on the throne. Between 1757 and 1765, Clive and his soldiers received about £2 million in 'gifts', and in 1765 the Company received the Diwan (tax collecting rights) of Bengal. From these secure foundations the Company was able to seek out new markets and sources for trading products.

Although the Company had failed to set up a lasting trading post in Japan, they were amongst the first to penetrate that most closed of nations, China, and the burgeoning demand for tea back home provided a steady revenue stream, supplemented by the trade in cottons, silks and porcelain. As European interest in the products of the East Indies increased, so the Company caused native designs to be modified to suit western tastes – porcelain and silks from China, and carved ivory, textiles and shawls from India were adapted to suit the new market, or sometimes they were specially commissioned for a customer back in England.

The profits from the China tea trade went some way to offset the costly military campaigns that, much to the disapproval of the Directors in London, were considered necessary to maintain the Company's hold in India. The principal enemy at the end of the eighteenth century was Tipu Sultan of Mysore, a Muslim ruler in a predominantly Hindu south Indian kingdom. Tipu was the sort of ruler who under any other circumstances the Company would have found exemplary. Religiously tolerant and fair-minded, he encouraged the development of the infrastructure and industry of Mysore, ran a fiercely loyal and effective army and was a generous patron of the arts. Unfortunately, he was also virulently anti-British, and had vowed to sweep them into the sea. A series of four Mysore Wars culminated in his defeat and death at Seringapatam in 1799, which gave the Company control of the southern Indian peninsula.

The arrival of Richard Wellesley as Governor-General in 1798 heralded another costly era for the Company, as he instigated the 'Forward Policy', the gist of which was that the extent of English influence should never abut that of an unpredictable power; which, given the prevailing situation in India at that time, called for unrelenting expansion. Wellesley was eventually recalled when he spent over £165,000 on a new Government House in Calcutta, modelled on Keddleston Hall in Derbyshire.

OPPOSITE **The Royal Stuart Coat of Arms on an Indian-made bedspread. Western designs were produced to order on Indian cloth and Chinese porcelain from the start of the Company's trading in the East.**

PREVIOUS PAGE
Government House, Calcutta, modelled on Keddleston Hall. 'A palace not a counting house'; its cost led to the eventual recall of the Duke of Wellington's brother.

RIGHT *Colonel Mordaunt's Cockfight* by Zoffany circa 1784. Not a stiff upper lip in sight. The highly cultured but decadent court of the rulers of Oudh at Lucknow attracted many louche European adventurers.

An Indian Maharajah once visited the original, and marvelled that the English should have bothered coming to India at all when they could have stayed at home 'playing the flute and watching the rabbits'. The Calcutta Keddleston represented the prevailing view of Wellesley's circle, including his friend Lord Valentia, that India should be ruled from a palace not a counting house, 'with the ideas of a Prince, not those of a retail trader in muslins and indigo'. Like an industrialist making his way in polite society, the Company was already starting rather to despise trade. Before he left, Wellesley had secured Delhi and with it the Red Fort containing the Moghul Emperor. The Company to which Jehangir had granted trading concessions two hundred years before now controlled the Moghul Empire itself.

The process of territorial expansion that started with Clive's annexation of Bengal, the 'private trade' which enabled merchants in the Company's service to make fortunes on the side, coupled with a high level of corruption, meant that more and more men sought their fortunes in India, and where the men went, women followed.

The easy-going lifestyle of the merchant adventurer in the Company's trading posts gave way to a more conventional society, with its clubs, churches, calling cards and social functions. Many of the accoutrements of civilised life had to be imported from England, and were adapted to suit the new circumstances. Wicker picnic hampers, tiffin and tonic water all evolved from the needs imposed by the harsh Indian climate. Hugely wealthy men returning from Company service to England attracted much envy as they bought up country houses and seats in Parliament, and many of these 'nabobs' kept the habits they had learnt in India. The rewards of India were great, but so were the perils, particularly disease, which laid waste many an ambition. The crowded English graveyards in India bear mute testimony to the short life expectancy there.

By the mid-nineteenth century the East India Company's writ extended across most of India, Burma, Singapore and Hong Kong, and a fifth of the world's population was under its authority. The Company had at various stages defeated China, occupied the Philippines, conquered Java and imprisoned Napoleon on its island of St Helena. It had neatly solved its perennial need for bullion to buy tea by conspiring illicitly to export Indian-grown opium to China.

It was the largest single commercial enterprise the world had ever seen, with revenues derived not only from trade but also tax-collecting. By an Act of 1833 the Company had been deprived of its trading privileges, and effectively became Managing Agent of India on behalf of the Crown. As it took on the administration of the fledgling Empire, the Company attracted men of evangelical zeal – Bentinck, the Lawrences, Edwardes – who saw their work in India as an

IX.

LEFT The missionary, aided by an interpreter, states his position to improbably enthralled natives. The Company had banned them from India up until 1813.

opportunity to introduce an enlightened regime in a country that had suffered under the yoke of previous conquerors. The constitution, the judiciary, and the education system of modern-day India owes a debt to these men, and the 'Company Bahadur (powerful)' they served. But this reforming fervour created the resentments which were to result in the Mutiny, as traditions were trampled over in the rush to enlightened rule.

Until 1813, the Company had forbidden missionary activity in India on the sensible grounds that it was likely to be disruptive. However, the evangelical movement, which had inspired the eradication of the slave trade, had other ideas. William Wilberforce, one of its prime movers, argued before Parliament that allowing missionaries into India (where he had never been) was 'the greatest of all causes, for I really place it before Abolition' and that 'our religion is sublime, pure and beneficent, theirs mean, licentious and cruel'. The Company reluctantly capitulated, and moral fervour became the engine of Imperialism. As Bernard Shaw put it: 'When he (every Englishman) wants a thing, he never tells himself he wants it. He waits until there comes into his mind, no one knows how, a burning conviction that it is his moral and religious duty to conquer those who possess the thing he wants. Then he becomes irresistible.'

One piece of 'enlightened' legislation that the Indians found particularly galling was the 'Doctrine of Lapse', brainchild of Lord Dalhousie, Governor-General between 1848 and 1856. By allowing local rulers to remain nominally independent as long as they didn't interfere with its policies and accepted the advice of the resident they installed, the Company was in charge of an India of which half the land mass and a third of the population was governed by independent rulers – the five hundred or so Princely States. By tradition, if the ruler had no natural heir, he could adopt one of his own choosing. However, Dalhousie regarded many of the rulers as degenerate and determined that their subjects would be better off under English rule. Consequently, he declared that in future when there was no natural heir the state would revert to the Company. On occasion, when he considered a ruler irredeemably given over to 'debauchery, dissipation and low pursuits' he would simply appropriate the state. When the vast and wealthy Kingdom of Oudh, hitherto an ally of the Company, was thus annexed, discontent became increasingly vocal, and the capital, Lucknow, was to become one of the centres of the Mutiny.

However enlightened they may have thought themselves, when the ruling English had become evangelised their great spiritual certainties often alienated natives of all levels. This was especially apparent in the Indian Army, where a situation previously based on a clear understanding between the employer and his mercenary forces became muddied by the English assumption of moral superiority and the implicit racism that came in its train.

Sensitivities and taboos that would previously have been respected were ignored, and the notorious issue of the cartridges greased with pig and cow fat was the spark that lit a tinder-dry stack of accumulated grievances.

The Mutiny was never a coordinated rebellion against the Company Raj; it was confined mainly to the Gangetic plain, never touched Bombay or Madras, and was immediately snuffed out in the environs of Calcutta. There was no clear native leadership, and no clear strategic aim beyond a vague yearning for the restoration of the Moghul Empire. Muhammed Bahadur Shah Zafar, the last of the Moghuls with the reduced status of King of Delhi, was the confused figurehead for the mutinous sepoys converging in Delhi from Meerut (where the Mutiny started in June 1857) and Agra. There were acts of extreme savagery, notably the slaughter of over 200 English women and children in the Bibigurh – an enclosed courtyard for women – at Cawnpore, which elicited deep pools of crimson prose from the Victorian press of the 'make the hoarse thunder of our guns sweet music in our ears' school. There were also fine examples of extreme British stoicism, such as at the famous siege (twice relieved) of the Residency at Lucknow, during which the 'soft and milky rabble of womankind' endured privations not anticipated even in *Tropical Trials*, the memsahibs' handbook. As the press excelled itself in overblown propaganda, the numerous English atrocities were transmuted into acts of righteous revenge. The Muslim inhabitants of the Old City of Delhi suffered enormously, and the gratuitous destruction of parts of the Red Fort despoiled one of the Moghuls' greatest architectural achievements.

The anomalous situation of the East India Company ruling a subcontinent – termed by Macaulay as 'the strangest of all governments for the strangest of all Empires' – could not last. After the Mutiny of 1857 was suppressed, it was obvious that a Company in which shares could be bought and sold was not the appropriate form of government for such a vital British interest. The India Act of 1858 saw the Company replaced by the Crown. Its final demise came in 1874, when its last Royal Charter finally expired. *The Times* reported: 'It is just as well to record that it accomplished a work such as in the whole history of the human race no other company ever attempted and as such is ever likely to attempt in the years to come.'

RIGHT **The Residency at Lucknow. Scene of a memorable siege during the 1857 disturbances, still touchingly preserved.**

From Company to Crown

Although the change from Company to Crown appeared monumental from the British end of the telescope, from the Indian end there was no appreciable difference. Ruled by English law underwritten by an English Government and an English army (albeit that many natives were in its service), the substitution of John Company by Queen – later Empress of India – Victoria, was for most Indians an incomprehensible technicality. Victoria's image in two or three dimensions had decorated most government buildings and city squares for many years, so there was little to signal change. No riots ensued, no heads rolled and revolutionaries failed to stalk the corridors of power. However, there had been a significant change in the relationship between the rulers and the ruled. The Mutiny had shattered the assumption that the

BELOW Delhi Durbar, 1877. Celebrations to mark the accession of Queen-Empress Victoria. The starving millions of the Deccan were not invited.

British were somehow destined, through innate superiority and exclusive access to a proper Christian deity, to rule the heathen masses of India. It showed that when push came to shove power had to be exerted through the most conventionally brutal of means, implacable and bloody. *Droit de seigneur* had to be ruthlessly asserted, and every mutineer was blown to pieces at the mouth of a cannon undermined the unconscious English belief in their God-given right to rule. The strict racial divisions exemplified by the Crown Raj in part reflected an attempt to suppress that new-found fallibility.

Having finally shown themselves to be good old-fashioned Imperialists, the British adopted high empire mode with a vengeance. Some measures taken were a common-sense response to the issues thrown up by the Mutiny: the ratio of British to sepoy (native) troops in the Indian Army was reduced from 1:9 to 1:3 to render it mutiny-proof, and no sepoys were to receive artillery training. All evangelical talk, with its implied threat of forcible conversion, was unofficially expunged from official communiqués, and Victoria announced that Britain had 'no desire to impose Our convictions on any of Our subjects'.

The 'Doctrine of Lapse' was allowed to do precisely that, and, although Oudh's monarchy was not restored, the maharajahs and nizams of the Princely States once more felt secure in their thrones, their loyalty during the Mutiny recognised. By 1876 things had settled down sufficiently for Victoria modestly to accept Disraeli's proposal that she should become Empress of India. In 1877, outside Delhi, on the Ridge that had seen so much action in the Mutiny, the new order was invested at an Imperial assemblage, to which 84,000 people were cordially invited, including many of the remaining independent Indian rulers.

Unfortunately this tamasha took place at a time when an appalling famine had broken out in the Deccan, claiming five million lives. The contrast between conspicuous display and rampant starvation was not lost on the emerging Nationalist movement in India.

No longer encouraged to convert their subjects, the British set about modernising them. The advances the nineteenth century had made in engineering and science were deployed in India with extraordinary energy, and, as fast as they could build them, railways, roads, irrigation canals and telegraph lines began to enmesh the land – an eruption of infrastructure that was known disparagingly as 'trains and drains'. Their subjects scrupulously censussed, their domains meticulously charted, their forests cleared and planted, the British could look complacently down from their borrowed Olympus (Everest had by now been shown by the English to be the world's highest mountain, although it was inconsiderately to be found in Nepal) and declare that it was good. Rather, as to this day Britain over-relies upon the highly specified infrastructural legacy of the Victorians, India has inherited the colossal results of this Imperial zeal; the stations may be heaving with the crush of humanity, and some trains may carry as many people outside the carriages as in, but every Indian railway passenger has reason to thank that implacable British single-mindedness of purpose.

The Company had presided over the last great phase of English expansion in India in the run up to the Mutiny with the annexation of Sind and the Punjab in the 1840s, the latter as result of two bloody wars against the Sikhs. Peace of a sort having largely been imposed on the whole subcontinent, the British military were able to amuse themselves with the machinations of the Great Game against the similarly formidable Russian Empire in the high Himalayas, and the army could be kept trim fighting the incorrigible tribesmen of the North West Frontier. A second Afghan war ended as scrappily as the first, and when Lord Curzon, Viceroy between 1898 and 1905, initiated the British invasion of Tibet under the leadership of Francis Younghusband, it seemed an anachronistic Imperialist gesture, and the desultory campaign was reflected in the indifferent, if not hostile reception the news received back home. In India, at least, the steam seemed to have gone out of the virile expansionism advocated by Wellesley at the beginning of the nineteenth century, and the countdown to Independence was well underway.

The outpouring of Indian support for the departing Lord Ripon, Viceroy from 1880 to 1885, was prompted by his resistance, albeit failed, to change the Ilbert Bill. In its original form it would have put Indian magistrates, in certain cases, in a position to pass judgment on English men and women. In expressing common cause with Ripon, the educated Indian classes suddenly found a collective voice, and were inspired to convene the first Indian National Congress in Bombay in 1885. The Congress was founded by a Scot, Allan Hume, a former Collector of Etawah and Commissioner of Inland Customs, the first of many non-Indian supporters of home rule. His theosophist colleague, Annie Besant, was a vociferous President of the Congress Party in 1917. As Gandhi later showed, politics and spirituality were never far apart in India. The 1885 Congress started the tentative discussions concerning Indian independence and the only thing that united the various parties was the issue of British oppression, and, as Hitler was later pithily to observe, 'there are Indians who won't kill a louse, so they won't kill an Englishman either'. Thus it took some time before sufficient consensus emerged for the Congress to coalesce into something resembling a political party, by which time the Muslim faction, representing some 20 per cent of the population, was already disaffected. In the meantime, the Diamond Jubilee of 1897 had allowed Victoria's far-flung subjects the opportunity to pay due homage in London, to the intense curiosity of her little Englanders.

LEFT Victoria's Jubilee, 1897. London's first sight of the Queen's more exotic subjects. This was perhaps the acme of Empire.

The sight of Maharajahs parading the streets in obeisance to the Queen-Empress was for many the apotheosis of Empire. By the time of the Delhi Durbar in 1911 George V was sufficiently secure in his possession to venture there himself, something that Victoria had never done.

The contribution of the Indian Army during the First World War is testament to the fact that the British had managed to rebuild loyalties which had been severely tested during the Mutiny. Over a million and a half Indians fought, and thousands of soldiers born on the plains of Punjab perished in the Flanders mud. Their sacrifice was an eloquent plea for the cause of Indian independence, which proceeded to gather momentum, only to be brutally suppressed

ABOVE 'So this is all mine? . . .'. George V surveys his domain with Queen Mary from the Red Fort at the Delhi Durbar in 1911. The first time an Emperor of India had set foot on Indian soil.

OPPOSITE A quiet ceremony. A procession approaches the Jama Masjid, India's largest mosque, from the Red Fort during the 1911 Durbar.

by the British authorities, particularly in the notorious massacre at Amritsar in 1919. The Punjab was something of a political hotbed at the time, and demonstration had been outlawed. This was sufficient justification, as far as Brigadier General Reginald Dyer was concerned, for him to order his troops to open fire on an unarmed crowd in the Jallianwal Bagh in Amritsar, killing 379 and wounding over 1,200 men, women and children. No other event since the Mutiny so revealed the widening chasm between the rulers and the ruled.

Although he resigned, Dyer was never punished, and he was lionised by the hardliners in the white community, and called the 'Saviour of the Punjab' in Britain. Indian Nationalists were appalled by this, and the Independence movement took on a more radical hue. Like the massacre at Cawnpore, to which it stands in curious counterpoint, Amritsar was a defining moment in the British Imperial adventure, when it stood under the world's gaze stripped of conviction and morally bankrupt. During the six minutes of continuous fire ordered by Dyer, India symbolically gained its freedom.

The Congress Party, and the rise to prominence of Gandhi and Nehru, gave hope to Indian Nationalists that the British might eventually be persuaded to grant them independence. There even appeared to be a grudging recognition of this at the highest political level in London. The fact that the Muslim component was largely missing from Congress made an overall political solution elusive, and the idea of an independent Pakistan started to take root. Lord Curzon, Viceroy from 1898 to 1905, had forced through the partition of Bengal in 1905, which prefigured the partition of Independence in 1947. Bengal had a majority Muslim population in its rural east, and Curzon's idea was to create, through partition, a new administrative province. Although not sinister in intent, it was imposed without consultation, and as result negatively perceived, leading to boycotts of British goods, rallies and some outbreaks of communal violence. It was reversed in 1911. The failed Bengal partition created a precedent which was ultimately to be followed on the grander stage of the subcontinent itself.

The continuous agitation by Congress culminated in the Salt March of 1930. It was conceived by Gandhi – a politician whose saintly air concealed a sure populist instinct – as a way of openly flaunting what was seen to be an example of British oppressiveness, namely the Government's control and taxing of the salt trade. Gandhi led the three-week march from his headquarters in Ahmedabad to Dandi on the Arabian Sea. By the time he had walked the 250 miles, his original entourage of seventy-eight people had swelled to a motley parade of village headmen, dancers, disciples, schoolchildren – and the world's press. In a symbolic gesture which was flashed around the globe, Gandhi picked a lump of salt from the shore; it was later auctioned for 1,600 rupees. Salt became the metaphor for a nationwide campaign of civil

ABOVE Churchill's 'half naked fakir' maps out the route to Independence with Nehru, newly appointed President of Congress, Bombay 1946. An extremely wily politician, Gandhi was by no means as simple as he appeared.

disobedience and demonstrations which left the authorities unable to respond in any other way than the usual repression and imprisonment. Within a year, over a hundred thousand Indian Nationalists were in jail, including most of the Congress leaders, as well as Gandhi.

Lord Irwin, Viceroy between 1926 and 1931, was a religious man who thought he understood Gandhi. After releasing him from jail, he took the unprecedented step of inviting him for direct talks, 'not as a Viceroy, but as a man'. The location was to be the recently completed Government House in New Delhi. Conceived as a new capital twenty years before in the full flood of Imperial pride, New Delhi was the architectural expression of a British vision of itself

ABOVE Masterful inactivity: the statues of the once-mighty rulers mourn the passing of the Raj in the Victoria Gardens, Bombay. After Independence their public places were taken by images of Shivaji Gandhi and other local heroes.

which had all but evaporated, and Government House, bigger than Versailles, was that vision cast in stone. Over a series of eight meetings, Gandhi, wearing a dhoti and a shawl and carrying a stick, would be watched by the press as he was swallowed by the immensity of the Lutyens building, to emerge some hours later after a cosy chat with Irwin in his study to walk home again. The talks themselves were inconclusive, but the symbolism was undeniable. As Churchill put it in his grandest Imperial style, he was revolted by 'the nauseating and humiliating spectacle of this one-time Inner Temple lawyer, now turned seditious fakir, striding half-naked up the steps of the Viceroy's palace . . . to negotiate on equal terms with the representative of the King-Emperor'. When, later that year, Gandhi came to England, not surprisingly Churchill refused to meet him.

By the time of the Government of India Act of 1935 Indians were allowed limited autonomy through provincial elections, with thirty-five million voters enfranchised. Congress was successful at the 1937 elections, capturing half the seats. However, this caused some panic amongst the Princely States, which suddenly woke up to the fact that their independence, effectively underwritten by the British since the Mutiny, would not necessarily be likewise guaranteed by their newly-elected compatriots who ironically viewed their 'debauchery, dissipation and low pursuits' with the same jaundiced eye as had Dalhousie. The writing was indeed on the wall for the Princely States, which were all absorbed around the time of Independence. The Muslims also felt threatened, and the term 'Congress Raj' was coined. Despite the suspicions, there seemed for a moment to be a genuine possibility that a phased withdrawal of the British could be safely achieved. The Second World War and Winston Churchill put paid to that.

Churchill's inspirational wartime leadership was born of an ardent Imperialist nature which even during the 1920s was regarded as distinctly old-fashioned. In the darkest hours of the Second Word War his bulldog Britishness maintained the home nation's morale, but he could not abide the notion of Indian Independence. When pressed to talk to some Indians to get a different perspective on Indian issues he retorted: 'I am quite satisfied with my views on India, and don't want them disturbed by any bloody Indians.' He dragged his feet in the ongoing diplomatic negotiations taking place there, and this brought into question the reliability of the Indian Army, then dealing with the threat of Japanese expansion through Burma. By alienating the Indians politically, the British were in danger of losing a vital military resource of two million men. The activities of Subhas Chandra Bose, who formed an independent Indian Army in alliance with the Japanese, never really manifested a serious military threat but were indicative of the fragility of the British hold in India.

Roosevelt had continually pressed Churchill to address the issue of Indian Independence, and after peace returned to Europe he could not avoid it. Weakened beyond measure, burdened by debt and with its soldiers simply wishing to return home, Britain had no appetite for continuing its Imperial adventure.

The Muslims, a fragmented political force up until the war, had used the hiatus it created to forge a credible political party, the Muslim League. The leader, Jinnah, advocated the creation of a separate state of Pakistan, encompassing the west of the subcontinent plus what is now Bangladesh. Despite the opposition of Congress, the tragedy that was Partition was cobbled together in haste, the opportunity for a solution that could have kept the subcontinent united having been squandered in the terrible struggles of the war. On 14 August 1947, the new state of Pakistan (including then East Pakistan, now Bangladesh) was formed, and at midnight on the same day British rule of the subcontinent came to an end, under the watchful eye of Lord Mountbatten, the last Viceroy of India. Predictably, the creation of East and West Pakistan by

Partition did not last very long. The domination by the West was to some extent a hangover from the old army recruitment mentality of the British after the Mutiny, where they preferred recruits from the 'martial races' from the mountain regions of the north-west, and as a consequence West Pakistanis were already heavily represented in the newly formed Pakistan Army, whereas the Bengalis from the East hardly got a look in. In 1955 East Pakistanis represented only 1.5 per cent of army officers. The higher ranks of the administration were similarly skewed in West Pakistan's favour; all of this was at a time when East Pakistan was producing 60 per cent of Pakistan's export earnings. The East Bengalis naturally considered that they were the victims of colonial oppression, and by 1970 they had the political will, in the form of the Awami League, to fight back. When the West tried to annul the results of an election, in which the Awami League won virtually all the seats allocated to the East, war broke out.

Since it depended upon the goodwill of India for the successful prosecution of its war of Independence from Pakistan in 1971, relations between the two countries have been considerably better than those between India and Pakistan. Bangladesh's principal problem is its repeated inundation, and the loss of life and economic havoc thus caused. The prospect of sea level rising as a result of global warming is a real and terrible threat to the welfare of what is already one of the poorest and most densely populated countries on earth. Only 6 per cent of its population of 120 million are considered adequately nourished, and 10 per cent are severely malnourished.

Elizabeth I's signature on the Charter of the East India Company in 1600 had given rise to one of the most extraordinary eras in human history, and 347 years later, it came to a close. England had taken the vast and disparate subcontinent and forged an Empire out of it, united under the yoke of English law, English language and Englishmen. Independence became inevitable, and regrettable as Partition was, and appalling the human cost – some twelve million refugees took flight, of whom large numbers, were slaughtered – it is perhaps remarkable that even more than fifty years after their departure, the subcontinent harbours only three nations. To stretch an analogy used by Nehru in his autobiography, the grand Imperial edifice that was India has suffered the fate of many a great house. The family who occupied it for a long time could no longer afford the upkeep and left; the central portion was taken over by the butler, who kept the name and most of the state rooms, and the later west wing was sold separately to the gardener's family. Sadly, the two neighbours don't get on at all, although they used to rub along together very happily in the old days. The damp east wing is home to the family of a cousin of the gardener's, who are rather poor and pretty much keep themselves to themselves. They got tired of him meddling in their affairs, and relations between the east and west wings are distinctly frosty. Occasionally, the original owners, now living in reduced

ABOVE British troops leave India in 1947. They marched through Bombay's 'Gateway of India', built to welcome in King George V, to board the last boats out.

circumstances on a run-down crowded estate at the other side of town, drop by to reminisce about former glories and get on the nerves of the occupants with their talk of how wonderful it had all been – the glittering balls, the shooting parties, the sense of space, the droves of servants . . . and as they leave, commenting on the state of the rosebeds, if they look back with half-shut eyes, they can see the house as it once was: a united India.

II

TRADE

The fine stonework
of the Diwan-i-Khas in
the Red Fort, Delhi was left
intact after the siege during
the Mutiny, barring the
precious stones prized loose
by British bayonets.

Traders & Colonists

Nothing remains of the East India Company's first toehold on the subcontinent, the factory established in 1608 at Surat on the north-west coast. Some of the walls could be seen until quite recently, but have since been destroyed by flooding; however, an English graveyard survives as testimony to the longevity of the factory, if not its occupants. This factory was far more than the word conveys today. Constructed on a standard model used by the Company throughout the East, it was a combination of warehouse, fort and an Oxbridge college, a secure base in which goods could be stored, prayers held, meals eaten and sleep taken. There was good reason to have all these facilities located together, for the Company's settlements were a magnet for its enemies: the one at Surat, established in 1608, was frequently under assault from jealous Jesuits, marauding Marathas and machinating Moghuls. It is a testament to the foresight of its founders that it survived remarkably well until the rise of Bombay, 150 miles to the south, in the late seventeenth century, undermining its trading importance.

If the embattled outpost of Surat represents the first phase of the Company's development, the second stage is embodied by Fort St George at Madras in the south-east. Here a small parcel of land was ceded by a treaty in 1639, enabling the Company to erect a permanent settlement, including a larger fort than the typical factory, as well as a church and other official buildings. With the fort as a secure bolthole, English traders and Indians alike had the confidence to move their homes outside the protective walls of the fort. Although the buildings have been altered over the years, nearly four centuries later the basic layout of Fort St George is much as it was even now, giving a clear impression both of the scale of operations of the Company and of how vulnerable they must have felt on that once lonely bit of coast.

RIGHT The East India Company's factory at Surat circa 1680. The first step in the creation of the Indian Empire. Permission was granted to trade here by the Moghul Emperor Jehangir.

1
3
4

RIGHT Fort St George. In 1639, the site of what is now the city of Madras was the Company's first territorial acquisition in India, and the fort was the first building established there, with many subsequent additions.

ABOVE Custom House Willingdon Island, Cochin. An entirely artificial island constructed during the 1920s to create additional docks, making Cochin one of the principal ports of South India.

Neither Madras nor Calcutta was blessed with a natural harbour, and both owe their status as major ports of modern India to the English initiatives to create access for oceangoing vessels. Likewise, the port of Karachi on the opposite coast, once a fly-blown fishing village, was conjured from the sand bars and spits of the Arabian Sea by significant engineering efforts; and in Cochin, the whole of Willingdon Island was constructed to create the required docks. Calcutta's Fort William was destroyed at the time of the Black Hole in 1757, but the reconstructed version, a state-of-the-art exercise in the science of fortification, survives to this day, having never been taken. Similarly, at Madras, the security provided by the fort enabled the town to expand enormously around it.

The East India Company – a trading company which developed into a trading empire – was indisputably the first and foremost practitioner of globalisation. Its avowed intent, as set down in its Royal Charter of 1600, was to increase 'our navigation and advancement of trade of merchandise' might seem removed from such weighty moral and political considerations as the abolition of suttee, the 'Doctrine of Lapse' and the merits of the 'Forward Policy' (as opposed to Masterful Inactivity), but all Imperial practice is founded on the principle that absolute

power should assert itself absolutely, whether in terms of land revenues, constitutional reform, education for the natives, territorial ambitions or the abolition of heathen practices. Despite protestations to the contrary, it is clear that an unswerving sense of racial, moral and spiritual superiority is the *sine qua non* of a mature imperialist world-view. This is perhaps why so many in Britain were shocked by Gladstone's late-nineteenth-century observation – seemingly self-evident according to Christian doctrine, and today positively politically correct – that the life of an Afghan peasant woman on a snowbound hillside in the Hindu Kush had as much value as that of any Englishman, comfortably ensconced in Havelock Crescent, Croydon. Thus Religious Enlightenment, Justice, Infrastructure and Good Government became the Imperial leitmotifs, the lineaments in which the profit motive could be displayed to good advantage and the applause of all on the right side of the colonial divide. Paradoxical as it may seem at first glance, it is a small wonder that the unabashedly rapacious traders of the Company's glory days in the eighteenth century enjoyed a more harmonious relationship at all levels with their subject peoples than the high-minded do-gooders of later years, for there is no greater bar to mutual understanding than hypocrisy. At root, trade was the motor of the Empire, and some aspects of trade remain its most lasting monument. The 1852 'Mofussil Directory' included the following in its listings for 'manufactories in Bengal': 8 collieries, 320 indigo factories, 3 distilleries, 2 iron works, 3 jute works, 1 ropery, 9 silk producers, 6 sugar producers and 34 tea plantations.

The relative significance of these commodities varied over time. Indigo, the original organic source of the blue dye used to colour military uniforms and now chemically synthesised to dye denim, was a very substantial plantation business for the English. This was until the 'Blue Mutiny' of the 1860s when production fell victim to the greed of the European planters, whose attempts to enforce potentially ruinous contracts on the native cultivators rebounded when the latter understandably refused to comply. Jute, used principally to make rope and sacking, was the foundation of Dundee's wealth and it is still a significant industry in Bengal. The trade in cotton today, cultivated widely in the Deccan, Gujarat and both Indian and Pakistani Punjab (Pakistan produces nearly half the subcontinent's output), took off after the outbreak of the American Civil War sent American production into a steep decline. It formed the basis of Bombay's relatively late prosperity: the city's still thriving Sassoon Docks, named after a Baghdadi Jewish trading dynasty, were built on cotton wealth. Coffee was introduced to India by a Muslim pilgrim, Babu Budan, in 1695, but it was not until the 1840s that the English started actively to promote its cultivation. Two commodities above all, both substantially developed by the English and both of which have prospered until the present day, will serve as examples of the trading imperative; one a shining trophy, the other, a poisoned chalice: tea and opium.

LEFT The docks of Karachi, the principal port of Pakistan, were created off the unpromising beaches of a tiny fishing village.

Tea

No single commodity has a stronger association with the East India Company than tea. The Company may have been founded to trade in spices, but 400 years later it is tea that is the most lasting commercial memorial to the British in India – not only because of the huge amount the subcontinent produces, but because of the even vaster amount that it consumes. From the Khyber to Cox's Bazar, and from Kashmir to Cape Cormorin, tea is an omnipresent part of life, regardless of religion, language, caste or culture. More than any other imposition of the English, tea has been eagerly adopted by their former subjects.

Originally, however, tea was an accidental discovery stumbled upon in pursuit of quite different ends. From their first attempts to gain entry into the spice trade, the Directors of the East India Company were aware that the constant drain on bullion reserves resulting from their activities was politically unpopular at home. Ideally, they would have liked to sell English woollen broadcloth to a third party in exchange for bullion, and then use that bullion to buy the spices which were the main target of their early trade. Recognising that the inhabitants of the tropical East Indies were unlikely to show much interest in their woollens, they looked north to the virtually unknown lands of China and Japan in search of markets. In China they encountered fierce opposition to their presence; in Japan they discovered tea.

It was John Saris, a thirty-two-year-old employee of the Company at its factory at Bantam in Java, who first suggested in a report to the directors in 1608 that Japan represented a fine commercial opportunity. Armed with copies of the charts originally stolen by the Dutch Jan van Linschoten's from the Archbishop of Goa, Saris was commissioned to take a ship from the Eighth Voyage, the Clove, and to set out from Bantam on a reconnaissance mission to Japan with the aim of establishing a factory there. When finally arriving in Hirado (a small island off the west coast of Kyushu) in 1613, he acquired the appropriate permissions from the Shogun in Yedo (Tokyo), and the English commenced trade. Just two years later, the first use of a word relating to tea in the English language is recorded, when in 1615 a Company factor, Mr

RIGHT A tour of duty for Indian troops at the world's highest frontier battleground in Kashmir does not preclude the taking of tea.

RIGHT A European merchant haggling over prices in a tea packing factory in Canton. The green leaves are trodden on in order to open the cell structure up to oxidation, creating black tea.

OPPOSITE A silver teapot presented to the Directors of the Company by Lord Berkeley in 1670. Specific brewing technology for the new beverage had not yet evolved, and so it closely resembles the commonly-used coffee pot.

Wickham, wrote to his friend Mr Eaton in Hirado asking him to buy a 'pot of the best sort of chaw in Meaco', the district where tea was grown for the Shogun. There is further evidence from letters between other Englishmen that tea drinking was well established amongst them in Japan even at this early date, half a century before a matrimonial alliance between the royal houses of England and Portugal set the scene for its rapid and enthusiastic adoption in England.

In 1623 the Company had closed its failing factory in Japan but, conscious that there was a potentially large market for this new and exotic drink, looked elsewhere for a source. It was hoped that the new demand could be met from China, which thus far had resisted the Company's advances. Tea had been used in ancient China for many thousands of years, and more than likely was drunk in Burma and Siam also – at first used for medicinal purposes, then later as a beverage. The Japanese had learnt the art of tea cultivation and drinking from their neighbour in the twelfth century. Russia was the first European nation to import tea, on camel trains across the Gobi desert; the tea was compressed into bricks for easy transportation, and the round trip from China took three years.

A little tea reached England via the private trade of the Company's servants – the 'China Drink' was mentioned in 1658 in an advertisement for the Sultaness Head Cophee-house in the City. In 1661, the Directors of the Company, anticipating the new commercial opportunity that tea represented, conducted a tea tasting at East India House organised by Sir George Smith, and decided 'good tea (to) be provided for the Company's occasions'.

When in the sixteenth century the Portuguese had established their trading post at Macao at the mouth of the Pearl River, they had taken up the local custom of tea drinking, and in due course transmitted it back to their homeland. In 1662 the English Stuart King, Charles II married Catherine of Braganza, a Portuguese Princess, and it was probably she who introduced the English court to the esoteric pleasures of tea, learnt in her native country. The East India Company, like any modern corporation, made use of exotic gifts as a way of influencing important people, and as it was keen to maintain cordial relations with the Crown – after all, its Charter required regular renewal – so the royal family received particular attention; none more so than Charles. In 1664 a returning captain reported to the Court of Directors of the East India Company that their agents in the East Indies had failed to make provision for the King; they scoured the ship for a suitable gift, and the minute book records: 'The Governor acquainting ye Court that ye Factors haveing in every place failed ye company of such things as they writt for to have presented his majesty with and that his majesty might not find himself wholly neglected by ye company, he was of the opinion if ye Court thinck fitt that a silver case of oile of cinnamon and some good tea, be provided for that end.' It is known that this is the first time that the King had received tea from the Company, although he certainly knew about it from his wife. It seems to have been a popular gift, for within weeks of the tea being given to the King, the Company ordered a hundred pounds of the 'best tee procurable' from its Bantam factory. Basking in the glow of royal patronage, within a short time tea was hugely popular in England.

Fortunately for the Company, the Manchu Emperor of China at last proved receptive: in 1685 Chinese ports were opened up for foreign trade. Ideally placed to make money from the new fashion, by 1687 the Company was selling sufficiently at home to be able confidently to place an order via Bombay to Amoy, the Company's first trading post in China, for 20,000 pounds of tea 'extraordinarily good, being for England'.

The tea trade with China rapidly assumed enormous significance, and from the mid-eighteenth century onwards was far and away the most important element in the Company's commercial activity. Canton, a port on the Pearl River upstream from Hong Kong and Macao, proved to be well placed to service the Company's requirements, and it established a factory there. By 1750 the Company was shipping over 2.5 million pounds of tea annually; at auction in London it could comfortably fetch five shillings a pound, at least twice the cost price in Canton. Swingeing duties, sky-high prices, smuggling and adulteration all failed to dent the ever-rising importation of tea, and fifty years later at the turn of the century over twenty million pounds a year were being sent back to England. By this time the tea trade produced more revenue than the whole of India; the humble leaf of *Camellia sinensis* was more commercially important to the Company than all the pomp and circumstance of the Raj.

The teas exported from China to Europe and America in the seventeenth and beginning of the eighteenth centuries were predominantly green (unfermented) teas, and were called curious names – most now disappeared – such as Hyson Skin, Bing, Caper and Twankay (after which Gilbert and Sullivan's Widow Twankey was named). Black Souchong and Congou teas became increasingly popular in England, as well as the most expensive Pekoes.

With tea in a position of such pre-eminence in the Company's commercial activities, it was inevitable that ways should be sought to circumvent the stranglehold of the Chinese on the trade. As early as 1788 Sir Joseph Banks, President of the Royal Society, the leading economic botanist of the day and consultant to the Company, recommended to this end that tea

ABOVE The balcony overlooking the fine garden of the Company's Canton factory was the envy of the other European traders. Hog Lane, behind the factories, was frequented by whores, thieves and hooch vendors.

plantations be established in India. If this project were to succeed, Chinese brains would need to be picked; hence, when Lord Macartney led a trading and diplomatic mission to Peking and the Chinese Emperor's summer palace at Jehol in 1793, the enterprise was bankrolled by the Company to the tune of £80,000. The mission may have failed to achieve its principal objective of better regulating trade at Canton, but it did give its participants an opportunity to study China more closely than any westerners before. The mission included an artist, William Alexander, to record the scene, and Macartney's secretary Sir George Staunton, an eminent botanist. Before the mission left for Peking, Banks briefed his friend and colleague Staunton to observe carefully and record the Chinese methods of tea cultivation, manufacture and scenting, and Staunton's report on his findings in China, edited by Banks in 1796, contained the first published general observations of this nature. The mission also brought back tea plants, which were successfully introduced in the Calcutta Botanic Gardens.

Although the Company had ceased to trade in tea with the much-debated loss of its China trade monopoly in 1833, it had not entirely lost interest in the plant. In its new patrician role as colonial administrator in India, the Company felt that it should encourage private enterprise to do what it might previously have done itself. Unconfirmed observations suggested that native tea bushes grew in Assam in north-west India, but it was not until 1834 that the then

OPPOSITE TOP LEFT Preparing the ground for new tea bushes in Assam.

OPPOSITE CENTRE LEFT The estate manager's house, Assam. Classical styling combined with corrugated iron roof and iron pillars.

OPPOSITE BELOW LEFT Shopping mall, Dibgugarh, Assam.

LEFT Good quality tea requires hand-plucking, and no viable way has been found of automating the process. Tea estates are thus still as labour intensive as they were under the British.

ABOVE Infant tea bushes are cared for in the nursery.

Governor-General, William Bentinck, took the initiative and formed a tea committee which belatedly discovered that 'the tea shrub is beyond all doubt indigenous in Upper Assam . . . within the Honourable Company's territories', and that the discovery was 'by far the most important and valuable that has ever been made in matters connected with the agricultural or commercial resources of this empire'. G. J. Gordon, a member of the Committee, was dispatched to China to secure tea plants, and experienced Chinese coolies were employed to supervise cultivation and manufacture. He returned with some 80,000 seeds, which were germinated at the Botanic Gardens in Calcutta. Eventually 20,000 seedlings were sent to Assam, but they did not fare well, and the Assam tea industry is now based on the indigenous type which had proved to be suited to cultivation during Gordon's absence in China. After a number of false starts, in 1838 twelve chests of Assam tea were shipped to the Court of Directors in England; on 10 January 1839 eight were auctioned at Mincing Lane, London, to much interest among both the trade and the public.

The same year of 1839 saw the first amateur efforts at tea cultivation by Dr Cambell, the Company's superintendent in the newly acquired Darjeeling district. Experimenting with seedlings from the small-leaved Chinese plants in his garden, he found that they thrived at high altitude; indeed, the results were sufficiently encouraging for commercial plantations gradually to be established. The acquisition of more territory by the Company in 1850 led to the further development of tea plantations. Darjeeling, and in particular those estates at an altitude of more than 5,000 feet, still produce teas of a quality greatly sought after internationally today, from plants derived from the Chinese stock.

Also in 1839 the Assam Company became the world's first tea company. Taking two-thirds of the experimental stations developed by the East India Company on a free ten-year lease (not quite the bargain that it might seem, for these plantations, often no more than jungle clearings, were spread far and wide, as the Company had sought to demonstrate that the tea could be cultivated over a wide area in Assam), they raised £500,000 in capital to finance the establishment of further plantations. Most of these funds came from London, but there were also some Indian investors. The Assam Company received its own Royal Charter from Queen Victoria, but, despite being well-financed and spending substantial sums on equipment and management, divisions between its London and Calcutta directors led to conflicts which dogged its progress.

In many ways the resolution of these corporate issues provided a pattern not only for the subsequent commercial development of the tea industry, but for many of the great private initiatives, particularly the railways, which were shortly to follow. Key issues were incorporated,

PAMBANARTEA FACTORY

previous page Tea Factory at Ootacamund. The heart of the tea estate is the factory where the fresh green leaves are fired, crushed, torn and curled to prepare them for the worldwide market.

right Coffee gets the thumb's down at this Calcutta tea merchants.

such as the way in which the end of the Company's trading role required the development of private-sector initiatives; the way in which investment was balanced between London and India; and, crucially, the way in which local management was given sufficient authority to deal with problems effectively. Thus, the Assam Company was an enormously useful testing ground for many of the key structural economic issues which faced the Victorian Raj.

The Assam Company itself was sufficiently profitable by the late 1850s to encourage many similar ventures, laying the foundations of the phenomenal growth of the Indian tea industry in the latter half of the nineteenth century. This expansion was assisted by the Company-sponsored mission into Bohea, China, by Robert Fortune, who returned in 1851 with seeds and detailed observations of tea growing there. At the time of the Mutiny in 1857 Indian tea exports scarcely register in the statistics; just twenty years later they had overtaken those of China.

In addition to Assam, which remains the most important of the tea-growing regions of India, by 1860 the first plantations had been established in Travancore, the Nilgiri Hills in the south, in the Kangra Valley in the north-west, in Darjeeling, Terai and the Dooars, and in Chittagong – modern-day Bangladesh. By that date India was producing in excess of a million pounds of tea annually. Today that figure has reached 850 million kilos, a commercial success story matched only by the phenomenal rise in consumption of tea. India alone manages to consume 640 million kilos of tea a year, and Pakistan and Bangladesh are also both heavy tea-consuming nations, although Pakistan has no plantations and those in Bangladesh produce only limited quantities of rather low-quality teas.

The tea industry in India (and, for that matter, the whole world, except China) has inherited the plantation/factory model fine-tuned by the English for the development of tea in Assam. That in turn was an amalgam of general plantation practices pioneered by the Dutch in the East Indies, predominantly Java, and on the Company's own plantations at Bencoolen on the south coast of Sumatra. All subcontinental tea plantations are orientated towards the production of black (fermented) teas, which now utilise heavy equipment for rolling and cutting the tea leaves, opening their cells up to the oxidation process. The first machines for this operation, which was originally done by hand, were developed in the 1860s, along with machines for drying the green leaves.

The popularity of black tea is in part due to the fact that its manufacture is easier to mechanise than that of green (unfermented) tea, which remains more of a labour-intensive, cottage industry in China, where it is mainly produced. The Assam plantations nevertheless employed vast armies of labourers, called 'coolies': Thacker's *Indian Directory* for 1885 has a helpful table for the calculation of coolies' wages, so a planter could quickly ascertain that to employ 9,000 of them would cost him 2,307 rupees, 11 annas and 24 pais a day.

The layout of a modern tea plantation would not be unfamiliar to an Indian planter from over a hundred years ago, and some would say that prevalent employment practices are equally outmoded. However, significant progress has been made among more enlightened plantation owners in the introduction of health and education programmes for their workers, as well as environmental schemes and, in some cases, organic cultivation.

The London Tea Auction, which held its last sale as recently as 1998, was the principal market of the world trade in tea until the mid-1970s as a result of the colonial pattern of large-scale tea growing, initially in India and later also in Ceylon (Sri Lanka) and East Africa. With the means of production secured within an Imperial framework of management and finance, it was possible for the British also to control the marketing and distribution of tea in the largest consumer market, the UK itself. The London Tea Auction was a direct descendant of the auctions at the old East India Company House in Leadenhall Street, and the progress of both reflects the rise and fall of commerce in an Imperial context. Initially a large variety of goods sourced in the East were sold by the candle at Leadenhall Street; then, increasingly, merchants in England began to specify the kind of goods they wished to be supplied. Eventually, one commodity, tea, became so important that it warranted its own auction, and in turn spawned an industry in the Eastern colonies to feed the growing demand back home, financed in part by the same traders who bought the tea at auction. Finally, Independence broke the magic circle; and, while the wheel of commerce continued spinning for some years, eventually the trade realised that the position of London at the hub had lost its meaning and purpose. The financial risk involved in shipping tea at some expense to be sold at fluctuating prices on 'spot' market was a decisive factor in the demise of the London auction.

Tea consumption in the subcontinent today reflects a healthy diversity of tea culture encompassing both the light green tea delicately flavoured with cardamom, which is preferred by the wild tribesmen of the North West Frontier, to the ubiquitous 'chai' brewed in boiled buffalo milk and spiced with garam masala served throughout the plains. In Ladakh, in the high Karakorum mountains, the Tibetan fashion of drinking tea flavoured with rancid yak butter can be enjoyed although, whether as a result of an absence of yaks or for some other reason, it has never caught on anywhere else. Most tea is still sold unbranded through the bazaars; but gradually even this most ubiquitous of consumer products is falling under the spell of modern marketing, and increasingly is sold pre-packaged under heavily advertised brand names.

RIGHT **It is hard to envisage Indian life before the English introduced tea and biscuits.**

Opium

Before the seeds of success for a native tea industry had been sown in India, the East India Company was still financing the purchase of huge quantities of tea in Canton. This presented a particular difficulty: the Chinese insisted on being paid in silver bullion, and, as there was no significant export trade to China, once paid the bullion went out of circulation. In an endeavour to recoup some of its funds the Company had for some time been involved in the opium trade, exporting the drug to China for cash payment.

In the seventeenth and eighteenth centuries no opprobrium was attached to the cultivation or consumption of opium, the narcotic properties of which had been widely appreciated since ancient times. Its use was already fairly common in India when the first Company traders arrived, and it was the favoured recreational drug of the Moghul Emperors Humayun and Jehangir. The Chinese, however, had an 'unbelievable passion' for opium, according to a French traveller of the 1770s, a taste they had hitherto gratified with supplies chiefly from Persia or Turkey. Turkish opium smuggled into China had been the foundation of John Jacob Astor's fortune; later he confined his sales only to England, where prominent figures such as Keats, de Quincey, Coleridge and Elizabeth Barrett Browning all fed their febrile imaginings with the drug. Finding that Indian-grown opium was of a higher quality than Persian or Turkish, the Company set about exploiting its advantage. From 1781 it took charge of organising opium production in India, and in 1793 declared itself the monopoly trader.

The opium produced in India was sold at auction in Calcutta to private merchants, who exported it to China in amounts rising from 1,000 to 4,000 chests of about 150 pounds weight every year. Officially, the Company had nothing to do with its destination; in reality, they knew full well where it was going. New edicts banned opium absolutely, but in China 'There was no pretence at enforcing them in the spirit' and 'irregular dues' were levied to ensure the connivance of the 'Hoppo, Viceroy, Governor, Treasurer, and so on down the list'. Lord Macartney had been briefed to tackle the problem of the opium trade on his 1793 mission; the Company wisely acknowledged that nothing should be done to put its vital tea trade in jeopardy, and that, 'useful as the opium revenue was to India, it was less to be desired than the China trade monopoly'. The Mission failed to resolve the issue, and the opium trade remained at the same level through to the 1830s, representing under 5 per cent of the annual Indian revenues of the Company – significant, but scarcely vital.

After 1830, however, there was a dramatic rise in Chinese consumption of the drug, and suddenly the Company realised the extent to which it had itself become quietly hooked on

Previous page Tallying opium balls in Patna in the late eighteenth century. Indian opium was declared superior to that of its Turkish and Persian competition. India is still the world's largest producer of licit opium for the pharmaceutical trade.

opium revenues. Meanwhile the Chinese government was debating the perennial issue of prohibition versus legalisation; for a while the private traders were gloomily predicting that the legalisers would win the argument. Eventually, in 1837, the Chinese Emperor took his strongest action yet: a total clampdown on the trade. Cantonese opium dealers were strangled in front of the foreign factories *pour encourager les autres,* and as the tempo escalated, leading Hongs were arrested. Stocks were ordered to be surrendered, and when only token amounts were collected, threats were made against Lancelot Dent, a leading private trader implicated (rightly) in opium smuggling. Captain Elliot, the Crown representative in Canton who was broadly sympathetic with the ban on the trade, ordered that all opium in private traders' hands be surrendered, and over a thousand tonnes, valued at £2 million, were burnt on the banks of the Pearl River.

It might all have ended in a wrangle over who should pay for the opium: the traders thought that they should be compensated by the Crown, as they were acting on Elliot's orders, while the Crown harboured hopes that the Chinese Government could be prevailed upon to pay. But the Canton Governor Lin, buoyed up by the apparent ease of his victory over the foreign barbarians, began to ratchet up his demands to an extent that Elliot could not countenance. Although the British Government accepted that the Chinese had a sovereign right to ban opium from its territories, it was not to be forced to the negotiating table; and so, in 1839, 3,000 men were sent to make 'war on the master of one third of the human race'.

The term 'Opium Wars', coined by *The Times,* was a catchy title for a conflict that certainly concerned the opium trade among other things, but was much more about trade than about opium; there is no evidence that the English fought for the right to impose opium imports on a suppliant Chinese Empire. Whatever the motive, the outcome was decisive. A small British army and a small naval fleet, supplemented by some Company steamers, prevailed over a Chinese Empire full of an anachronistic sense of its own importance. Fragmented and weakened by internal strife and misrule over decades if not centuries, it was in no condition to resist the terms imposed by the humiliating Treaty of Nanking in 1842, which forced the opening of the 'Treaty Ports', including Shanghai, to foreign trade. Military defeat of the Chinese provided the opportunity for the British to seize access to Chinese territory not in pursuit of Imperial expansion, as in India, but for commercial activity. The most significant provision of the Treaty of Nanking was the cession of Hong Kong to Britain. The events leading up to the Opium Wars had forcefully reminded both the British Crown and the British private trading interests that Canton was by no means a secure location, prompting resumption of the perennial search for such a base, which had been going on intermittently for as long as the Company had traded with China. During the war, Captain Elliot had sheltered from a Chinese attack in the harbour of Hong Kong island, and was convinced that it was the most

ABOVE The capture of Chinkiang during the Opium Wars, which were less about opium than the compulsory imposition of free trade.

suitable choice. Although Formosa, Amoy and Chusan were also considered, in the event the choice fell on Hong Kong, and although it was a Crown rather than a Company territory, it was a logical extension of the Company's involvement in China for many years.

By the late nineteenth century, however, England and America were themselves attempting to control domestic consumption of opium and its derivative, morphine. The Saint James Society in the USA commenced the free distribution of heroin to sufferers of morphine addiction, with the unexpected result that heroin addiction grew alarmingly. Illicit opium production in the Shan States on the fringes of British Burma, which had commenced in an attempt to circumvent the lucrative Government monopoly, was brought under a measure of control. But India continued to produce prodigious quantities. In 1906 some £2.25 million, 7 per cent of the total income of the Government of India, was derived from opium. Hong Kong's economy, as well as its population, was highly dependent on it, and it was to popular outcry that the dens were closed in 1907. Even Crown officials were not unsympathetic: the Governor of the

LEFT Coleridge's poetical inspiration became the foundation of a multinational criminal industry: the opium harvest in the North West Frontier, Pakistan. Much opium is also made in Afghanistan, helping to fund the fundamentalist Taliban regime.

colony, Sir Frederick Lugard, made a personal tour of inspection of what he preferred to call 'divans', and found the scenes of 'animated and intelligent' opium smokers there more endearing than those in a comparable London public house.

In 1911, opium stocks worth £12 million were threatened by a renewed Chinese Government crackdown, and banks and merchants pressurised the Government to force the Chinese to abide by the consumption levels in a previous ten-year agreement, even though India was still producing at a higher level than had been deemed acceptable by that agreement. Although opium was considered highly unhealthful in Britain and America – it had been banned by the US Congress in 1905 – evidently the Chinese constitution was inured to it. Henry Keswick, the former Tapipan of Jardines, showed himself a fine politician when answering parliamentary concerns at Westminster as Member for Epsom: he defended opium as the Chinese equivalent of a glass of beer or wine, which he would not be alarmed to find his sons imbibing – beer or wine that is. Despite all the heated debates in Parliament, the Hong Kong Government took the opium monopoly into its own hands with such embarrassing success that in 1918 the proceeds, at $8 million, represented half of the total government revenue. Such was the huge vested interest in the maintenance of the trade that it took the Second World War and the Japanese invasion to dislodge the colonial authorities from their dependency, and opium was not finally proscribed in Hong Kong until 20 September 1945.

In their cultivation and forcible distribution of opium the English had effectively established a working model of what is now called the drugs trade. Today, the two principal sources of illicit opium and its derivatives are the Shan States and the tribal territories of the North West Frontier in Pakistan – both areas which at the height of the Empire were under British control. While it would be unjust to blame nineteenth-century British practices for every junkie in Washington Square today, the fact remains that by industrialising the production of opium in India, and enforcing the 'free trade' in the drug to China, the British had clearly set economic interests above a nation's narcosis.

The Americans played new variations on the British theme in the 1950s and 1960s, when their fear of communism in South East Asia caused them to make unholy alliances with heroin warlords, leading to a massive influx of heroin into the USA. In India itself, opium production is now heavily policed, and the subsequent shift of illicit opium cultivation to the tribal territories can be seen as no more than a commercial necessity. It is now estimated that 80 per cent of the heroin in the UK and 30 per cent of that in the US, comes from this area; the Taliban's control of Afghanistan is in part financed by the trade.

Shops & Markets

The bazaars or markets of Asia have always been legendary in their size and diversity. The Great Bazaar in Kabul was the finest of all until it was blown up by the English in retribution for the First Afghan War. It was inevitable that the noisy, dirty and disorderly bazaars of India would be viewed with distaste by the fastidious English. Hence, shopping areas reminiscent of the English high street sprang up in the cantonments and around Company and colonial settlements. Usually called the Mall, this haven of shaded walkways giving into cool and tranquil shops was where the memsahib could be looked after in the style to which she was accustomed. Many of these cantonment shopping areas still survive, and although they have been infected by the pace and squalor of modern India, they often retain a residual calm from their British days.

In the cities, of course, there was not the luxury of such space. Calcutta was well stocked with shops and department stores from the mid-eighteenth century, and the Esplanade and Chowringhee Road are still among the main retail streets of the city. Bazaars were reinterpreted by the Victorians with the creation of covered markets in the tradition of hundreds of English towns and cities. The finest examples can be found in Bombay with Crawford Market, which is decorated with sculpted figures by Lockwood Kipling; and Calcutta, where Hogg Market has been compared to its counterpart in Huddersfield.

New Delhi's, Connaught Place, is a series of concentric circuses in which many of the best shops are still to be found. It resembles an uneasy mixture of Rome's Colosseum, Bath's Circus and the wedding-cake fantasies of a half-crazed confectioner. The complex has managed to cope with the pressure of the motor car and Coca-Cola hoardings.

LEFT AND RIGHT
Crawford Market, Bombay. The exuberant bazaars of India harnessed by the Victorian British love of order.

S·A

above When the Royal Enfield motorcycle factory in Redditch closed in 1970 production continued in Madras. The Bullet retains a certain cachet in the Japanese-dominated Indian market. A new Indian-made Royal Enfield is available in the UK.

left The Austin Ambassador, derived from a 1950s English design, is still seen widely in India where it has been made in Calcutta since its inception.

LEFT Imposing and authoritarian, the building in Bombay appears as solid and reliable as the bank it houses.

III

THE ARMED FORCES

The view the Moghul
Emperors enjoyed from inside
the Diwan-i-Khas,
Red Fort, Delhi. It was built
by Shah Jehan, who later
constructed the Taj Mahal.

THE COMPANY ERA

Although the Indian Army represents the most significant and conspicuous military legacy of the Raj in the subcontinent, it should not be forgotten that the navies and air forces of India and Pakistan, and later Bangladesh, were also inherited from the British. It is salutary to reflect that when the armies of Pakistan and India clash, as they have done all too frequently since Partition, both forces involved were founded by the East India Company. The Indian Army (in the subcontinental sense) has been called 'a military anomaly' for this reason, but there is a strange logic to the emergence of one of the largest standing armies on earth from the boardroom of a London trading company.

The Company's Raj in India has been called a 'garrison state', in which the military underwrote commercial and territorial ambitions. With at most 125,000 European men, women and children among a native population of 250 million inhabitants, the garrison must at times have seemed in a state of perpetual siege, but through a combination of skill, luck and unwavering self-belief, the conquerors managed to convince the conquered of their superiority. They would not have been able to do so without the support of the native soldiers of the Indian Army, and when that support was partially withdrawn, as it was at the time of the Mutiny, the vulnerability of the Raj was exposed.

The military organisation of the Company in India was complex; at any one time the Company might deploy native troops (sepoys) of its Indian Army; European troops of the same army; the British Army stationed in India and subsidised by the Company; forces of Indian princes or states in alliance with the Company; and irregular cavalry or troops formally or informally associated with the Company. These permutations were first successfully developed as a result of French activities in the Carnatic.

RIGHT **Uniforms, brass bands and regimental pride all descended from the Indian Army founded by the East India Company, on parade, Republic Day, New Delhi.**

RIGHT Bare feet and shorts did not prevent sepoys of the Indian Army from being the most feared fighting force in the subcontinent. Third Battalion, 1773.

Strategically, although the Court of Directors was opposed to military adventurism, at least in the early years, it was necessary for the Company's servants in India first to defend their trading factories, and then to make military alliances with local rulers to pre-empt possible attacks. There is a fine line between pre-emptive defence and attack, and that line was quickly crossed. In the mid-eighteenth century southern India suffered an extension of the struggles between France and England in Europe and North America. The formative years of the Indian Army were largely driven by the need to respond to the political and strategic exigencies of the war with France between 1740 and 1748 and, shortly after, the machinations of the French Governor of Pondicherry, Joseph Dupleix, whose cunning alliances with regional rulers threatened the Company's existence in the Carnatic. Thus, the interests of the Company and the Crown were mutually dependent: the Company needed additional military support, which was given to them by Crown troops, and the Crown couldn't afford to let France achieve supremacy in India or, for that matter, further east.

The French had pioneered the use of the sepoy, a word derived from the Persian 'sipahi', meaning a regular soldier, which was applied to native mercenaries. The English were initially unconvinced that they could make a viable fighting force, but often they were all that was available to make up numbers, and in time and with training, the sepoy became the mainstay of the Company's armies.

Initially, it was felt that there was no requirement for regular troops, until a farcical war was prosecuted against the Moghul Empire between 1686 and 1689. This left a few Crown troops at a loose end in Bombay; these troops joined with the Company's own troops, the new sepoy regiments and with the allied armies of local rulers, to ward off the French threat in south India.

In 1756, the Company-founded town of Calcutta was attacked and occupied by Siraj-ud-daula, Nawab of Bengal. He was determined to prevent Europeans from gaining a secure foothold in Bengal. He ordered that both the Company and the French should stop fortifying their settlements. The French complied but the English did not, so the Nawab destroyed the newly built defences. The resultant 'atrocity' became known as the 'Black Hole'. This was revenged by Robert Clive, who had earned his spurs against the French, at the head of the nascent Company Army he had forged there. The only Crown regiment to serve in Bengal was the Dorset Regiment, which still carries the motto 'Primus in Indis'. The Battle of Plassey, which could not have been won without the treachery of Mir Jafar, the Nawab's first minister, was the first outing of this Bengal Army. However, its real test was its decisive victory at Buxar in 1764. With the Diwani in Bengal to protect, the Bengal Army outgrew the smaller armies in Madras and Bombay. The Council in the latter seemed to feel their Presidency was a poor relation of the others, and unwisely embarked on a spot of empire building of its own. The first Maratha War in 1779 ended ignominiously when the Bombay Expeditionary Force was harried from the field by the light, flexible Maratha cavalry. To rub salt in the wound, the Governor-General Warren Hastings had had to send troops over from Bengal in belated support.

OPPOSITE **'Skinner's Horse' at exercise circa 1840. The use of the lance from horseback is still practised in the sport of tent pegging.**

Whilst the Directors of the Company could, with persuasion, see the justification for paying for permanent infantry to defend their burgeoning Indian interests, they drew the line at cavalry, believing that superior artillery and small arms combined with better-disciplined troops would be ample to deal with any threat. The fact that man for man cavalry cost twice as much as infantry would not have escaped the ever-parsimonious Directors, but officers in the field felt the lack of tactical flexibility. When the Company finally allowed cavalry, they were able to attract the Muslim recruits who had previously eluded them, leading to a religious imbalance in the armies that was felt to be a source of potential problems. In the nineteenth century, cavalry was often irregular, such as Skinner's Horse; this was built on the traditional 'sillidar' system, whereby the troopers provided their own horse and equipment. Another complication to the command structure was added by the local 'contingents', which were under the control of the civilian rather than the military authorities in some states such as Gwalior and Hyderabad.

The most significant opponent of the Company's expansion in the eighteenth century was Tipu Sultan, the 'Tiger of Mysore'. Tipu has become something of a protonationalist hero in modern India, and his insistence that tiger motifs were worked into his uniforms, cannons, cane handles, bed hangings, swords and thrones created a fine cult of tigerish personality around him which may in part account for his longevity in the popular imagination both in India and Britain. His humiliating defeats of the English and subsequent rumours of his harsh treatment of prisoners during the Second Mysore War caused widespread hysteria in Britain, and Cornwallis's capture of Tipu's capital, Seringapatam, in the Third War was greeted with universal (English) acclaim. The treaty Cornwallis imposed on Tipu involved his two young sons being taken hostage as a guarantee of good behaviour. They were taken to Madras and looked after with exemplary kindness – treatment that inspired artists to make patriotic flights of fancy in praise of Britain's 'benevolence and conquest'. In the Fourth Mysore War, which ended in 1799 with Tipu's final defeat and death (although his sons were once more led into captivity), the old enemy was finally laid to rest, with a similar outpouring of jingoistic fervour. His palace yielded the famous 'Tipoo's Tiger', now one of the most popular exhibits at the Victoria and Albert Museum.

For European officers, the Indian Army had many attractions. Unlike the Crown Army, commissions were not bought, or sold, but achieved on merit, which opened it to the ambitious sons of the middle classes. This meant that officers would try to make as much money as possible whilst on active service; the batta, or field allowances, were generous and exploited to the full, and backhanders on supply and transport were the norm. Prize money and other bounty further supplemented the regular pay. Crown officers may have been contemptuous of the social standing of their counterparts in the Indian Army, but their postings generally gave better opportunities to make substantial amounts of money, and the Company was a good paymaster. By 1796, regulations were enforced to give parity to Company and Crown officers, and to increase the number of European officers in the Company Army. The latter had the effect of stifling the higher promotion prospects of the most able sepoys, and contributed to the background noise of disaffection at the time of the Mutiny. Training for this new European officer class was facilitated in 1809 by the founding of the Company's cadet college at Addiscombe in Surrey.

The Indian Army was kept entirely for the defence of India, and made a number of forays abroad in defence of that interest. They marched across Egypt from the Red Sea in 1801 to take on Napoleon (who had already been beaten by another army marching from the

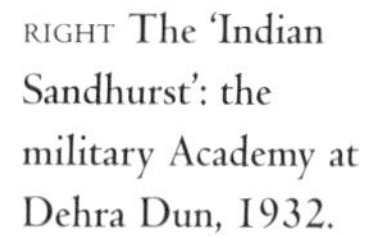

RIGHT **The 'Indian Sandhurst': the military Academy at Dehra Dun, 1932.**

ABOVE The 8th Bengal Cavalry in Marseille on the way to the trenches, 1914. The contribution of the Indian Army in both World Wars was enormous.

Mediterranean), invading Java in 1811, and seeing action in Burma, China, Persia, Arabia and Afghanistan during the Company's Indian rule. By this time the sepoy battalions rivalled in effectiveness those of the Europeans, and the Bengal Commander-in-Chief boasted that some of his sepoy battalions on parade '... would astonish the King of Prussia'. The famous Gurkha regiment was added to the Company roster as a result of the Nepalese War, although they were initially regarded by the explorer Hearsey as 'cowardly, shitten rascals'. He later modified his view and said that under the Company's guidance they might make 'excellent soldiers', which, once the Company had decided to extend their hospitality to the newly annexed Kumaon and Garhwal, they did, giving up their former allegiance to the King of Nepal and taking the Company's rupee. Originally Mongolian but more recently from an area to the north-west of Katmandu, the Gurkhas were small, tough fighters. Armed with their lethal 'kukri', a machete-like sword, they became a mainstay of the Company's army in the north-west, and are to this day one of the British Army's most respected brigades. Some three regiments were adopted by the British, leaving a further seven behind in India after Partition. Recently, however, having fallen victim to defence cuts and the loss of their Hong Kong base, recruitment to the British Army's brigade of Gurkhas has fallen to about 200 men a year, and there are fears that many of these are Marxist infiltrators fomenting a 'People's War' in western Nepal against the constitutional monarchy.

The rapid expansion of the Company's Indian territories, initiated by the Governor-General Richard Wellesley's 'Forward Policy', continued unabated until the inevitable conflict with the Sikh kingdom of the Punjab. Under Ranjit Singh, a one-eyed opium addict of legendary guile and charm, the Sikhs had managed to avoid fighting the English. His death brought on a chaotic succession of disputes, and the well-armed Khalsa, the European-trained Sikh Army, was itching to take on the English. The First Sikh War gave the Indian Army its severest test of the nineteenth century, and the Battle of Ferozeshah in 1845 has been called 'the most terrible battle of British Indian history'. This was made more terrible by the leadership of the superannuated Sir Hugh Gough, who was unable to comprehend the purpose of artillery, even when that of the Sikh's reduced his staff to a pulp.

The conclusion of the Second Sikh War in 1849 brought about the final annexation of the Punjab, although the English had already come into contact with the wild and warlike tribes of the Afghan Frontier who required a completely different style of fighting force to deal with them. Thus was formed the 'Corps of Guides', which became the most admired and famous force in India.

At its height the Company's Indian Army consisted of 250,000 men, of which no more than 45,000 were European officers and men. There was no need to recruit sepoys forcibly; they were professional soldiers who served the Company in return for a livelihood, status, security and honour. They would often be small landowners, and the pay in the Company's service was good enough for a man to be able to send home two-thirds to support his family. He was able to employ a man to carry his bundle, and others to cook and look after him. Frequently, he came from the Rajput warrior class or high caste and pursued the role that his social status required of him, and would require of his sons. Loyalty was a matter of caste honour, not engendered by any particular merit in the Company, officers of which were alien in culture, temperament and habits. Nevertheless, partly through the passage of time, partly as a result of the success of the Company in the field, and partly through the personalities of the officers, there did spring up a deeper trust and loyalty, one which was abused during the time leading up to the Mutiny, and then fatally overestimated.

Part of the problem were the attitudes exemplified by the cantonment. Cantonments evolved a short distance outside existing cities, for reasons of security and drains, and were permanent military camps with all the civil amenities such as a club, a church and residential bungalows,

BELOW **Gurkhas of the Indian Army are put through drill during a rehearsal for Republic Day, New Delhi.**

laid out in generous shady streets. The rise of the cantonment coincided with the arrival of the memsahib, and reflected the increasing distance at which the English wished to maintain their subject people.

It was partly at the instigation of Lord Napier of Sind, whose concern for the welfare of his troops was legendary, that the British belatedly started to realise that the hills were not only a suitable place for recuperation, but that troops should be regularly stationed there as a relief from the heat and disease of the plains. Thus came about the military hill station, a more congenial version of the cantonment, freed by the topography of the grid-iron plan. The finest example is the Wellington Barracks at Jakatalla near Coonoor in the Nilgiris, still the home of the Madras Regiment. Unfortunately, the new initiative for the creation of these military hill stations was taken too late to lessen the accretion of grievances and resentment that had built up amongst the sepoys, particularly in the Bengal Army.

The Mutiny was by its nature a defining event for the Indian Army: never again were the British to place so much reliance on the loyalty of the sepoys, and the sepoys themselves realised that the British were not *au fond* the benign power they liked to think themselves. The battles of the Mutiny were of a scrappy, skirmishing kind, and the set pieces were the Sieges of Delhi, Cawnpore and Lucknow. The Siege of Delhi began with the British being besieged on the Ridge, then in turn besieging the mutineers in Shahjehanabad, the citadel known as Old Delhi. Other than General John Nicholson, who succumbed to a sniper's bullet during the successful attack, the engineers of the Delhi victory were precisely that: engineers. Lieutenant-Colonel Richard Baird-Smith, the Delhi Field Force's chief engineer, had spent the previous seventeen years building canals in the Punjab, and his assistant, promoted to 'Director of Tunnels', had previously worked on the building of the Grand Trunk Road. Between them, they designed and built tunnels, embrasures, trenches, ditches, fortifications and batteries, turning the area between the ridge and the city walls into an essay on mid-Victorian engineering techniques. They enabled the big siege guns to get close enough to bring down the walls, and for sappers to place the gunpowder that blew open the Kashmir Gate.

In fact, nearly all the great civil engineering projects of the mid-nineteenth-century Raj were designed and undertaken by military engineers. All except the railways – although Consulting Engineer Colonel J. P. Kennedy was responsible for setting many of the standard practices, including the system that bridges should be built so that they were capable of carrying double tracks, although only single tracks were laid. Roads and irrigation, the telegraph, the Survey of India, the Government Mints, the Police and the Medical Service were all predominantly staffed by soldiers.

The soldiers at the sieges of Cawnpore and Lucknow were likewise unorthodox. Civilians, clergy, women and children took turns to load the guns and mop the brows of the few professional soldiers left fighting. The hardships for all the besieged were stupendous, made doubly so by the heat of the summer, and their resistance legendary (although Wheeler at Cawnpore capitulated under the false promise of safe passage to Allahabad), but these were scarcely conventional military actions conducted by two opposing armies, which is perhaps why they have an enduring place in the popular imagination of British India.

With the suppression of the Mutiny came the demise of the Company. The Indian Army became a Crown Army; the ratio of sepoys to Europeans was reduced to 3:1 and artillery was entirely taken over by British soldiers, with the exception of mountain artillery. There was a shift both in the composition of the sepoys and their field of action. By 1914, 75 per cent of Indian Army sepoys were drawn from what were known as 'martial races' with a warrior tradition, which meant that increasingly the men came from the north-western fringes of the Empire – Sikhs and Pathans – or indeed, like the Nepalese Gurkhas, from another country altogether. Likewise, because of the Russian menace, the North West Frontier and its volatile tribes became the single most active part of India from a military point of view, and a rotation system was instigated whereby regiments would serve four years in the plains and spend two years garrisoned on the Frontier.

LEFT A neglected pillar marks the scene of the desperate struggle by the British to defend Cawnpore against the Nana Sahib during the Mutiny.

The Great Game

If there is one area of India where the fighting skills of the natives were widely admired, and where the British found themselves dealing with an intractable enemy who was possessed of courage and cruelty in equal measures, it was the North West Frontier. Lying on an ill-defined border between Pakistan and Afghanistan, the Frontier is a spectacular, harsh and unruly region which still exhibits many of the characteristics that made it the most feared area of the Raj – and the testing ground of the most skilled soldiers and administrators that the British could muster. Its position at the intersection of two spheres of influence – British and Russian – ensured its place in the history of the Raj, and whilst the details of the Second Mysore War and the victories over the Marathas – crucial as they were at the time – have long been forgotten, the very name of the Khyber Pass raises a frisson of half-remembered fear even today.

Although often attributed to Kipling, the phrase the Great Game was in fact invented by one of its prototypical players, Captain Arthur Conolly, who had to endure his last days in June 1842 in a pestilential pit belonging to the Khan of Bokhara. His last minute was spent defying an attempt to convert him to Islam before his head was removed by a scimitar. Such was the undoubtedly potent combination of British resolve and oriental cruelty that appealed to the Victorian Imperialist view of those who travelled off-piste in defence of British India.

LEFT Arthur Conolly lost his head in Bokhara in 1842 rather than embrace Islam: his last words to his executioner were 'Do your work'. All part of the preliminary manoeuverings for the Great Game.

RIGHT The Khyber Pass in the North West Frontier of Pakistan has disgorged more than its fair share of invading hordes on to the subcontinent.

PREVIOUS PAGE
A deceptively placid view of the Bolan Pass, the other traditional invasion route into India.

It took two Greats of Russia, Peter and Catherine, to lay the foundations of British paranoia concerning the imminent Russian invasion of the subcontinent. Their expansionist ambitions were well known, even though the anticipated route of their invading army through South Central Asia wasn't. However, it was enough to read in history that Darius of Persia, Alexander the Great, Mahmoud of Ghazni, Tamburlaine and the founder of the Moghul dynasty, Babur, had all found their way from the high Afghan plains through the steep defiles of the Khyber Pass to north India, for the Company to take care that the Russians didn't execute the same manoeuvre. Even the French were a threat – after Napoleon's brief conquest of Egypt there were real fears that he might be next down the Khyber. In 1809, to forestall such a catastrophe, the Honourable Mounstuart Elphinstone led the first Company mission to Afghanistan. He stopped in Peshawar, at the eastern entrance to the pass, where the ruler, Shah Shuja-ul-Mulkh, had his winter capital. Elphinstone was entertained in great style at the Bala Hissar, where he caught a glimpse of the renowned Koh-i-Noor diamond. He was disturbed to find that no sooner than the ink was dry on a treaty guaranteeing Afghan opposition to any French forces attempting to cross its territory, his host fled Peshawar in the face of a force assembled by his half-brother Mahmud, another claimant to the throne. This was a fair, if alarming, introduction to Afghan affairs, which were turbulent, treacherous and unfathomable at the best of times. Steps had to be taken to understand the uncharted, alien lands on the western fringes of India.

The first detailed military and geographical analyses of these unknown regions were conducted by East India Company officers in a variety of occasionally successful disguises. Christie and Pottinger went in to bat in Baluchistan in 1810 as Tartar horse dealers, and, when they later split up, they independently adopted the guise of Muslim holy men, each somehow surviving rigorous catechisms. William Moorcroft, the hero of many later gamers, opted to use his genuine expertise as a vet to oil the wheels of his expedition to Bokhara, whilst Conolly travelled the 4,000 miles from Moscow to the Indus disguised initially as a merchant but later as a doctor. Alexander 'Bokhara' Burnes explained to the curious, on his unprecedented journey in 1832 up the Khyber to Kabul and over the Hindu Kush, that he was an Englishman on his way home who wished to take in some of the glorious sights of Central Asia.

Company politicals and strategists poured over the secret results of these explorers' observations, and arrived at the conclusion that any prospective invader of India would have to deal with unruly Afghanistan first. When the Persians, encouraged by Russian advisers, started to rattle the gates of Herat in western Afghanistan in 1837, the Prime Minister, Palmerston, uttered his fateful words: 'If the Russians try to make them Russians, we must take care to make them British first.' Eschewing an alliance with the powerful Dost Mohammed, who had

ABOVE The Moghul Emperors dreamed of the cool air and clear streams of Kabul. Ruined since this photograph was taken, it is hard to know who dreams of it now.

been identified as the only Afghan capable of uniting the warlike tribes against a Russian invasion, the Governor-General of India, Auckland, sent the formidable 'Army of the Indus' up the Bolan Pass in 1839 to Afghanistan.

After placing the craven Shah Shujah on the throne in Kabul, the British complacently occupied the city, installing a race course, foxhounds – and local mistresses, much to the fury of the tribesmen. Burnes, the political deputy and an arch-womaniser, fell to a mob's knives in the Kabul bazaar in 1841, and by the end of the following January the game was up. Only one man remained from the once glorious invading force, Doctor Brydon, who limped from the frozen defiles into Jelalabad on a wounded pony. The dead from the Retreat from Kabul, one of the greatest defeats suffered by British arms, were commemorated in the Afghan Church in Bombay; the balmy, breezy Englishness of its location belying the chilling brutality of the deaths it recalls.

There was outrage in England and an 'Army of Retribution' battled its way up the Khyber, blew up the great covered bazaar of Kabul – the most magnificent in Central Asia – indiscriminately looted the city, and then allowed Dost Mohammed to return to rule as ably as he had always said he would. Although he briefly sided with the Sikhs against the British on the promise of getting Peshawar back from them, he was otherwise a considerate neighbour. His refusal to entertain Russian overtures at a critical moment during the Indian Mutiny of 1857 created breathing space in the Punjab which enabled reinforcements to be sent to the Siege of Delhi. He could thus be said to have been a staunch ally of the Company in its hour of direst need.

LEFT Dost Mohammed. The most capable leader in Afghanistan's history was ousted by the misguided British.

In the period between the two Sikh wars, the British started to get to grips with the politics of the Punjab. The 'Corps of Guides' were raised in 1846 in Peshawar by Harry 'Joe' Lumsden at the instigation of Henry Lawrence, the resident in Lahore. At the time the only police and army forces available for law and order duties in the Yusufzai (the plain of Peshawar) were Sikhs, who had a poor reputation amongst the local Pathans who had suffered under them considerably during the period of Sikh rule. For the heads of the new British regime to demonstrate their impartiality, it was important to have a force of non-Sikhs at their disposal, and Lumsden was given free rein in the creation of his Guides. He recruited locally, selecting the most rebellious types and moulding them through force of personality and example into a fiercely loyal and effective troop. There was soon a waiting list to join, and by the time the Guides had moved to new headquarters in Hoti-Mardan, between Peshawar and the Indus, they included Gurkhas, Sikhs and members of the wild border tribes in their ranks. They were to prove their worth at the Siege of Delhi during the Mutiny, and remain the most prestigious corps in the Pakistan Army.

From the outset, Lumsden chose to dress the Guides in loose clothes made of a cloth dyed a yellow-brown colour known as khaki, Urdu for 'dust', which made the troops harder to spot. The colour was quickly adopted by other regiments – the besieged soldiers at Lucknow improvised the dye from red and black office ink. Khaki has been called 'arguably the greatest contribution to the comfort and safety of troops, not just those of the British and Indian armies but to forces throughout the world'. It can now be found on the High Street as well.

In the relatively peaceful years that followed the Mutiny, the Great Game was conducted more in boardrooms than in the field. The British bought a highly strategic stake in the Suez Canal to secure the fastest route to India, and laid an undersea cable to secure communications. The Russian advance in Central Asia continued inexorably, and plans for a railway from the shores of the Caspian towards Afghanistan were mooted. However, it was the acceptance – albeit with great reluctance – by Sher Ali, Dost's successor to the Afghan throne, of a Russian mission to Kabul in 1878 that raised British hackles once more. They immediately demanded that a British mission, under the command of the urbane Major Louis Cavagnari, be accepted. To underline their demands they sent him to the border accompanied by 30,000 troops, which led inevitably to the Second Afghan War. The British had learnt the bloody lessons of the First Afghan War, and this time they didn't send all the troops to Kabul to protect the mission. In fact, they sent only seventy-five men, drawn from the Guides, with Cavagnari, so that when they were inevitably slaughtered to a man in an uprising soon afterwards, no ignominious retreat of thousands was necessary. The Army of Retribution was dusted down and sent to Kabul under General Frederick Roberts, who promptly hanged many guilty men, as well as

RIGHT A fort at the frontier between Pakistan and Afghanistan. Khyber Pass.

OPPOSITE Badges of the regiments that have fought in the Khyber Pass. The Frontier was a plum posting for an ambitious officer.

BELOW The Indus River traditionally formed a crucial barrier to armies invading India. Alexander the Great, having leapt over it on his magical horse Bucephalus, sailed down the Indus with his homesick troops, leaving India behind him forever.

NWF INDIA 1914_17
BAWANJA
1962 - 1963
1ST BN THE 22ND (CHESHIRE) REGT
1933
17
DOGRAS
1ST BN

many who were innocent, to a great chorus of disapproval back home. Another disastrous defeat for the British at Maiwand in 1880 led to a further glorious reprisal, and having achieved nothing but the placing on the throne of Dost's grandson, Abdur Rahman, who, ironically, had most of this time been in exile under Russian protection, the British retreated once more, not to return in force until a half-baked Third Afghan War in 1919.

The problems of the North West Frontier of India, peopled by the same ferocious, independent Pathan tribes who warred and won in Afghanistan, were those of a local kind. Having given up any idea of actively occupying Afghanistan, the British concern was to secure the border between India and that disorderly country. Unfortunately, the Pathan tribes had different ideas, and the legacy of the continual battle can still be seen, predominantly in the North West Frontier Province of what is now Pakistan. The so-called Tribal Territories, a strip of mountainous country following the border with Afghanistan, still exist to this day, still thrive on a diet of smuggling, drug cultivation, arms manufacture and are still a thorn in the side of their nominal overlord, the Government of Pakistan. Effectively a no-go area, in the Tribal Territories the authorities still have to be satisfied with the rule of law a hundred yards either side of their paved roads. Beyond that, anything goes, and usually does. Mud fortresses, home to local warlords, bristle with private militias armed with locally made mortars and captured Kalashnikovs. This anomalous situation was inherited from the British. The famous Durand Line, an idea of Sir Mortimer Durand, whose father had successfully blown up the gates of Ghazni in the First Afghan War, threads its way through the tenuous allegiances and ancient hostilities of the tribes of the Frontier in a remarkably enduring attempt to delineate this most fluid of borders.

Strategic passes are defended by forts – the most important being Jamrud, which still looms over the entrance to the Khyber Pass like a child's model – and the craggy hillsides are dotted with pickets, refuge from the notorious tribal sharpshooters. The Khyber was always the most likely invasion route into India, and as late as the Second World War measures were implemented to defend it; a network of underground concrete bunkers and gun emplacements was built there should Britain fail and the home Government, as was once contemplated, removed itself to its most precious possession.

The other route into India, the Bolan Pass, was effectively blocked by the establishment, by treaty with Sher Ali in 1876, of the garrison town of Quetta, north of the pass and not far from the strategic Afghan city of Kandahar. Built to cantonment design, Quetta is surrounded by harsh, dry mountains, a reminder of its proximity to Afghanistan. Its nearby hill station, Ziarat, still provides a cool retreat from the summer heat for provincial government officials of Baluchistan. Jinnah, the founder of modern Pakistan, died in the Governor's House there.

LEFT **A smuggler's mule train rides the Khyber Railway, the best maintained track through the pass.**

Once the Afghan issue was 'settled', in the sense that both parties decided that the country was more trouble than it was worth, the British and Russians moved the Great Game to the uncharted, mountainous areas of north India and the Pamirs, 'where three Empires meet', as it was described at the time – the third Empire being that of China. The relocation took place principally because of the completion of the railway line from the Caspian via Merv and Samarkand to Tashkent, which itself was made possible only by the Russian annexation of the Khanates of Bokhara, Khiva and Khokand. Only Kashgar, which, despite their vigilance, was recovered from the Muslim warlord Yakub Beg by the Chinese, prevented the Russians from effectively controlling the whole north-western border of India. However, the railway meant that they could pose a credible threat of shifting men and heavy supplies swiftly to the northern passes, making invasion via the troublesome Afghanistan redundant. The only problem with this was that no one really knew where the northern passes were, and when they were passable. Thus ensued in the last decades of the nineteenth century the strange game of high-altitude hide-and-seek immortalised by Kipling's *Kim*. The traces of this veritable cold war are few, although the immaculate, secretive mapping commissioned by the Survey of India of the northern wastes is still relied upon by the Governments of Pakistan and India. The explorers and politicals who ventured into these remote regions were almost by definition loners, travelling light and leaving no material traces, except the odd lonely grave, such as that in the Christian cemetery of Gilgit of George Hayward, Royal Geographical Society gold medallist, murdered at Darkot in 1870.

Occasionally the cloak-and-dagger work would threaten to spill out into the public arena, as when Russia claimed part of what had been generally accepted as Afghanistan, throwing out an English explorer, and an obscure one-yak village called Bozai Gumbaz became 'the Gibraltar of the Hindu Kush'. The Russians backed down, and a boundary commission came up with the ingenious solution of joining Afghanistan with China by an umbilical corridor – the Wakhan Valley. Only ten miles wide at times, Wakhan served the purpose of separating Russia and British India, making border incidents less likely. Wakhan remains part of Afghanistan to this day and until recently has been populated by Khirghiz nomads who were unable to roam in communist China and Russia. It served as a conduit for Chinese weapons and supplies during the Russian occupation, masterminded by the Khan of Wakhan, Rachman Qoal. The Russians may have thus regretted the pragmatic arrangement they made with the British at the end of the previous century.

The explorer whom they had ejected from Bozai Gumbaz was Francis Younghusband, one of the foremost exponents of the Great Game. He was the nephew of the renowned gamer, George Shaw, whom he revered. Younghusband was born into an Indian military family, but quickly found his niche in Intelligence, in which capacity he made a trip from Peking westwards into north-west India, crossing the Mustagh Pass in the winter.

BELOW A Khyber steam train carries the unwelcome prospect of Pax Britannica to the unruly Frontier tribes. The railways were seen by the British as an essential strategic asset.

He was then sent to negotiate with the Mir of Hunza, an unknown bandit kingdom, where he met a Russian officer, Gromchevsky, with whom he amiably compared Imperial notes. Younghusband was a complex character, part Imperialist and part mystic. He was to lead the controversial invasion of Tibet in 1903, experiencing a spiritual epiphany outside Llhasa, which may have explained his later espousal of strange causes such as the multidenominational Religious Drama Society. His movement in support of the First World War, the 'Fight for Right', is remembered chiefly for Younghusband's commissioning of a setting by Sir Hubert Parry of William Blake's 'Jerusalem'. The mystic poet's vision of Albion became the mystic Imperialist's most lasting legacy.

Throughout the climax of the Empire, the North West Frontier itself remained prone to outbreaks of insurrection at the drop of a turban. Miniature versions of the Army of Retribution that had been sent into Afghanistan were frequently sent on punitive raids to punish recidivist tribesmen who had contravened British law by failing to pay their taxes, reverting to banditry, committing extortion, kidnapping or killing – in fact, all the customary amusements which had occupied them for generations. Fifty-two major punitive expeditions were mounted between 1849 and 1908, as well as hundreds of smaller raids. The Frontier became the breeding ground for an unique brand of 'muscular Christians', such as John Nicholson, whose methods of exerting his will in the Bannu district were so unusually fierce that he earned the natives, undying admiration, and is commemorated by the Nicholson Memorial by the side of the Grand Trunk Road near Rawalpindi. He even enjoyed the distinction of having a sect, the Nikolsayns, devoted to him.

The Umbayla Campaign of 1863 was a typically Frontier 'butcher and beat it' encounter fought against Muslim fanatics in Sittana. It required 238 dead and two Victoria Crosses before the British were able to carry out their ritual village burning. Winston Churchill saw the action as a war correspondent during the similar Malakand Campaign of 1897, and a picket on that pass bears his name. He didn't fare as well as Viscount Fincastle of the 16th Lancers, who was acting as war correspondent for his rival, *The Times*: he won the VC. Even as late as the 1940s punitive campaigns, designed to reduce villages to rubble and peasants to penury, were conducted, although by this time the RAF were involved, it being infinitely easier to send in a few fighters to strafe a wayward valley than to attempt to move in overland. Nevertheless, with the British being in a more or less constant state of war with some part of its inhospitable terrain, the Frontier contributed to the battle-readiness and experience of the troops, and was regarded as a plum posting for any ambitious young officer hoping to make his mark, and thus provided many an opportunity for 'Two thousand pounds of education (To drop) to a ten rupee jezail'.

THE WORLD WARS

Under the terms of the Government of India Act which legislated the transfer of power from the Company to the Crown, a more precise definition was arrived at for the function of the Indian Army. In the Company's days the Army had become involved in a number of campaigns as far afield as the Philippines and Egypt. An informal agreement was usually reached whereby the Company would be reimbursed for the expense of sending its armies abroad if it was patently on Crown business. In this way the Indian Army came to be seen as something of an instrument of Imperialism, a mercenary force which could be deployed when and where British interests were at stake. This was not a situation that could be allowed to continue in the new order of things: now that the Crown and India were one, the fiscal and cost implications of the use of the Indian Army had to be fully clarified. As a result, it was determined that the Indian Army should be used for the defence of India against external aggression; for the maintenance of order within India, and deployed elsewhere only in an emergency. This redefinition became a very knotty political problem in the lead up to Independence, as it was patently not possible to give India its freedom unless it had the ability to defend itself, but the maintenance of civil order in those turbulent times depended upon British control of the army, which the Viceroy insisted should be at his ultimate command.

LEFT The 2nd Rajput Light Infantry enters Baghdad, 1917. Anything must have been preferable to the horror of Flanders.

Such issues started to be raised after the First World War, which was properly deemed an emergency, with the result that many Indian soldiers served, and many more enlisted voluntarily. Although the Frontier was a good training ground for guerrilla fighting, it hardly prepared Indian soldiers for the horrors of an industrialised European war of attrition, and the possible loss of half their comrades in a three day battle. The battles they fought in Europe had a decidedly lowering effect on morale, already sapped by homesickness and the unfamiliar equipment, the mud, the cold, and the exhaustion of Flanders-style trench warfare. Self-inflicted wounds became commonplace, and it was decided to redeploy the Indian infantry in the Middle East, whilst two cavalry divisions, better able to adapt to the new situation, continued serving on the Western Front until the end of the war. The disastrous surrender of an entire Indian Army at Kut, near Baghdad, in 1916 was blamed (posthumously) on the poor leadership of Kitchener rather than the fighting qualities of Indian soldiers. By the end of the war over a million Indians had served abroad: 650,000 in Mesopotamia, 150,000 in Egypt and Palestine and the same number in France, with smaller forces in Aden, Africa, Greece and Gallipoli; 60,000 were killed, and eleven Victoria Crosses awarded. In the context of the simmering resentment of the Nationalists in India, the Indian contribution to the British war effort, mainly through the participation of freely enlisted men, was remarkable.

The Massacre at Amritsar in 1919 quickly put paid to any idea that the British might be disposed to be grateful, and the army emerged as a focus of particular political attention. The announcement in 1923 that certain regiments could be 'Indianised' was but a faint move in the right direction, technically allowing the entire regimental command structure to be in Indian hands. The creation of an 'Indian Sandhurst' at Dehra Dun in 1932 was supposed to provide a new Indian officer class, but in fact only a few hundred KCIO (King's Commissioned Indian Officers) were in service by the outbreak of the Second World War. With the civil disturbances, principally caused by the Independence movement, becoming daily more disruptive, the British felt that they could not afford to lose control of the Indian army; the issue of relinquishing control was itself one of the causes of the agitation. The problem was compounded by the fact that the Indian police were no longer as reliably pro-government as before. Despite their anxieties to maintain appearances to the contrary, the British were increasingly starting to use the Indian Army as an army of occupation.

Meanwhile, the ostensible function of the army as security against external aggression continued in much the same way as before the First World War. The Third Afghan War was thought necessary in 1919 to deal with incursions prompted by the declaration of *jihad* by King Ammanulah. The Frontier occupied much time and resources, although increasingly the RAF was used to carrying out punitive raids on recalcitrant tribes. Planes would first drop leaflets indicating that they were about to destroy a village, and shortly afterwards they did so, with bombs, rockets and machine-gun fire. It was far cry from the gentlemanly viciousness which characterised the glory days of Frontier warfare. Another Islam-inspired insurrection by the Ipi in Wazirsitan took considerable effort to suppress in 1936–37. But none of these actions could cover up the fact that the main function of the Indian Army had shifted to that of maintaining internal security.

With the approach of the Second World War another unpalatable truth had to be swallowed; if the Indian Army was to be in a fit condition to defend the wider interests of the British Empire in the East, it had to be modernised. The eighteen cavalry regiments that still used horses, and the command culture were equally obsolete, indicating that serious improvements needed to be implemented. This was a political, as well as strategic problem; there was no way that the Nationalist movement would tolerate India paying for the modernisation of forces for defence of an Empire from which they were trying to cut free. The British decided to foot the bill themselves, and when the war finally broke out, once again the Indians responded magnificently. The Indian Army served in the Middle East, France, North Africa, East Africa, Greece, Singapore (where 70,000 of their troops were captured) and Burma. It was in recapturing the latter country that the Fourteenth Army, under General Slim, earned the most distinction.

As well as taking Burma, the Japanese had actually invaded India, at least southern Assam, and their strategy of cutting off access for the allies from India to China looked like it would succeed. They were assisted, albeit feebly, by the Indian National Division brought together under Japanese supervision by Subhas Chandra Bose, and made up principally of Indian prisoners of war taken at the fall of Singapore. The image of Indian fighting Indian on Indian soil under the respective flags of Britain and Japan is historically compelling, but ultimately the loyalty of the vast majority of Indians lay with the British. Bitter fighting at Imphal and Kohima led to the expulsion of the Japanese and Bose's Indians, and their gradual withdrawal down Burma, with the Indian Army under Slim (himself an Indian Army officer) harrying them at every turn. Some elements of the Indian Army had had some experience of jungle warfare in the glamorous, but rather unsuccessful service of the Chindits under Orde Wingate, and they were able to drive back the Japanese, who lacked any kind of coordinated air support.

Two and a half million Indian soldiers had served in the Second World War, the vast majority again volunteers. Independence was only two years away, yet they were happy to serve under the colonial oppressor, a fact that has been given scant recognition in most histories of the Second World War. There has been much discussion by historians of the relative contribution by the Russians and the western allies, but little is said about the contribution of the Indian

Army, which, given the prevailing domestic circumstances in India, was particularly significant. Although the civil disturbances were rife throughout India during the war, they required the attention of only a fifth of the infantry – the other four-fifths fought against Axis and Japanese aggression at least as valiantly as the British themselves.

After Partition, the 175 cantonments built by the British in the subcontinent were divided along geographical lines between Pakistan, India and Bangladesh. The traditions of the regiments they housed – the brass bands, the Mess dinners and regimental silver, the *esprit de corps* – still speak of their British origins. In Pakistan and Bangladesh, where the political structure was by and large an *ad hoc* response to the threat of a Congress Raj, the army, has frequently stepped into the political arena, representing themselves as the last bastion of order and efficiency in a mire of political corruption and nepotism. The army in India, by contrast, has managed to maintain an apolitical stance. One of the dangers of India's increasingly precipitate slide into Hindu Nationalism, corruption and caste wars is that the resulting civil disorder might require the intercession of the army at a political level; the example of India's neighbours should be heeded. The inheritance of the Raj lives on in all three countries, and whilst equipment and training has moved with the times, the language and traditions of the officer classes in particular still recall pre-Partition days. This can still be seen in the regimental parades, the uniforms and the fact that Pakistan is the world's largest producer of bagpipes.

RIGHT **A soldier does his bit for the Pakistani bagpipe industry at the Lahore Show.**

NAVY & AIR FORCE

The East India Company's naval force was based initially in Surat, and assisted undermining the threat of the Portuguese, gradually earning the respect of the Moghul and pirate forces alike. When the Marathas under Shivajee started in earnest to threaten to take Surat from the Moghuls in the 1660s, it was with some relief that the English decamped to Bombay, the new base that had been acquired by Charles II as a result of his marriage to Catherine of Braganza. The nascent navy was titled the Bombay Marine in 1687, having largely managed to avoid getting sucked into the battles between the rival Moghul and Maratha fleets. The Marine's small but effective fleet of nine frigates consisted mainly of ships built in India from long-lasting Malabar teak by Parsi shipbuilders who joined the English from Surat. These were augmented by 'gallivats', oared troop carriers with some armour which were well suited to the anti-piracy operations of the Marine: the coast below Bombay was indented with rivers and creeks that served as ideal pirate lairs, and the merchant shipping was severely disrupted by raids, particularly by the notorious Angrians. In 1756 the Angrian fort of Sevedroog was taken, and later troops under Clive, supported by a bombardment by the Marine, successfully stormed the stronghold of Gheriah.

The Marine had by this time gained such a reputation that it was appointed to the splendid position of Admiral of the Moghul's Fleet and the East India Company was paid some £10,000 per annum to escort and protect the pilgrim route from India to Mecca, a service it performed until 1829. Increasingly, the Marine became involved in charting the seas, and in this respect their legacy is unsurpassed; without their work the oceans between Aden and Canton would have remained uncharted, and the hazards to shipping unidentified and unrecorded. They also undertook surveys of great rivers, not only those of the subcontinent, but also as far apart as the Euphrates and the Irrawaddy. As the Marine started to grow in size so it also acquired the accoutrements of a proper navy – uniforms and its own Bombay Marine battalion – and it began to make its presence felt throughout the East, mounting operations as far apart as Perim, at the head of the Red Sea, and Ternate, one of the Dutch Spice Islands that had eluded the Company in its earliest years. European wars against the Dutch and the French found their echoes in the seas of the East Indies. In the same way as the officers of the Indian Army were resentful at the less than favourable terms that prevailed there compared to regular Crown troops, the Marine suffered in comparison to the Royal Navy. Sweeping reforms were introduced in 1830 to redress the balance, and the Marine was retitled the Indian Navy. These reforms coincided with the introduction of a radical new naval technology – steamships – on the world's oceans, which increased the power and the range of the navy.

OPPOSITE **The Chiefs of Staff of the Indian Navy and Air Force.**

The new navy quickly adopted the recently invented steamships, and by 1841 they had nine such ships in service. For a while the Marine ran an efficient 'packet boat' passenger service between the Red Sea and India, but it was in war that the new vessels proved their worth, supplying logistical support via the Indus for the First Afghan War and Second Sikh War, and taking an active, aggressive part in the Opium Wars in China, the Second Burmese War and the war against Persia in 1857. Despite its success the Royal Navy finally took over all its duties in 1863. Downgraded once again to the Bombay Marine and, later, in 1877, Her Majesty's Indian Marine, the rump of the old Indian Navy continued to provide coastguard patrols, troop transport and minesweeping functions until after the First World War, although always in the shadow of the Royal Navy. In 1934, the Royal Indian Marine once again changed name to the Royal Indian Navy. At the outbreak of the Second World War, it had a fleet of eight warships, which by the end had risen to 117 combat vessels and 30,000 officers and men.

After Partition it was necessary for both India and Pakistan to establish independent naval forces from the thirty-two ageing vessels left in the Royal Indian Navy. India has nevertheless built up a substantial navy based out of Bombay (Western Naval Command),Vishakhapatnam (Eastern Naval Command) and Cochin (Southern Naval Command). The Eastern and Western commands both have naval dockyards. Pakistan likewise has established naval dockyards at Karachi, and has built up a navy of limited strength to look after its relatively short coastline on the Arabian Sea. Both navies draw on the traditions of the Royal Indian Navy, and its various predecessors in title, including the Bombay Marine.

The Indian Air Force was officially incorporated in 1932, and, as we have seen, was active in support of punitive expeditions in the North West Frontier. By the outbreak of the war it had sixteen officers and 662 men. As with the other services, the war led to the rapid expansion of the IAF, for although RAF squadrons were posted to India, only the IAF could accommodate the volunteers that came forward. As a result training schools were hastily established and the IAF, by 1944 equipped with rather obsolete Hurricanes and Spitfires, was able to play a significant role in providing air support for Slim's Burma campaign. As a result of the Second World War the IAF had grown in strength to 28,500 men, including some 1,600 officers. At Partition, the IAF base in Peshawar and an experienced force was passed to Pakistan, which adopted the colonial mantle and continued to use the newly created Royal Pakistan Air Force as a way of keeping the unruly Frontier tribes in order. The PAF (having dropped the Royal on Republic Day in 1956) developed rapidly, and its officer training base at Risalpur, near Mardan, frequently took British flying instructors on secondment from the RAF, continuing the traditional connection between the Frontier and the British. In the meantime, the newly independent Indian Air Force had immediately flexed its muscles when, in October 1947, it

RIGHT **Hawker planes of the fledgling Indian Air Force flying over the Karakorum before the Second World War.**

acted in support of the military counter-insurgency actions in Jammu and Kashmir. The trouble over this region, which still continues today, had started straight after Partition when a substantial, though disorganised, body of Pathans had invaded the territory which had technically become part of India.

In the days of the united India, the chief strategic area of concern was the North West Frontier, through which traditionally the invaders of India had arrived. Pakistan having effectively taken over that troubled region, India no longer had any control over its defence, but a disastrous war with China in 1962 showed that there was always the opportunity to seek amusement elsewhere. By this stage the Indian armed services as a whole had become heavily dependent on Soviet equipment and support, and the link with the British was thereby considerably weakened. The creation of Pakistan was predominantly a reaction to the potential danger of a Congress Raj, rather than the result of a strongly politicised Muslim disaffection with the British presence in the subcontinent. The British in general had always felt more affinity with the monotheist Islam than with the strangely multi-faceted Hindu religion, and the Indian Independence movement was distinctly Hindu in character. To this day the armed forces in Pakistan have closer ties with their progenitor than their Indian counterparts, who have perforce shuffled off the colonial coil in a more determined and ideologically-driven manner. This observation can be extended from the military into the civilian sphere: other than fundamentalists, Pakistanis in general are considerably more relaxed about the historical British connection than Indians.

BELOW **Women officers (only recently admitted) of the Indian Air Force (inherited from the British) play snooker (invented by the British at Ooty Club, where women have not been admitted as members since it was founded).**

LEFT Fortunately, the grand ceremonial avenues of Lutyens' New Delhi are well-adapted to helicopter fly-pasts.

IV

RELIGION & REMEMBRANCE

Stained glass in
St Mary's in Fort St George,
Madras – the first Anglican
church to be built
on Indian soil.

Churches

When the Portuguese first arrived in India in 1498, a hundred years before the East India Company, they came not only as traders, but also as Christians – and particularly convinced ones at that. Their treatment of the heathens they encountered was frequently barbarous, and their desire to impose their Catholicism where they could was an unstoppable driving force. As a result, their old eastern capital at Goa on the west coast of the Indian peninsula has a heavily Christian culture. Hindu temples were destroyed, sacred lingams were broken up, and locals were forcibly converted as the Portuguese extended their territorial reach. The abandoned city of Old Goa is awash with monasteries and churches, reverting gracefully through humidity-stained whitewash to jungle, and the Jesuit missionary St Francis Xavier lies buried in a magnificent tomb of Italian marble in the Bom Jesus Cathedral. One consequence of the activities of the Inquisition is that sprinkled through the paddy fields of the province are fine little churches with well-scrubbed, active congregations. What was once a violent imposition has mellowed into an unexpected charm.

In contrast, it was no part of the Company's first charter to spread the word of God, and the exclusion of missionaries from India was a firm policy until 1813, when it broke under evangelical pressure. As far as the Company was concerned, God-fearing and prayerful as many of the merchants were, missionaries and trade did not mix. These attitudes are evident in the architecture of early English churches in India. Modest places of worship, like country parish churches back home, they were not built to convey the greater Glory of God to the uninterested natives. St Mary's in Madras was the first Anglican church in the East, snuggled within the protective walls of Fort St George. It was consecrated in 1680 and was designed by William Dixon, Master-Gunner of the Fort, who applied his profession to the task in hand. He saw to it that the church could usefully double as a fortress in times of need by making it virtually fire- and bomb-proof, and castellating it against armed uprising. The church builders

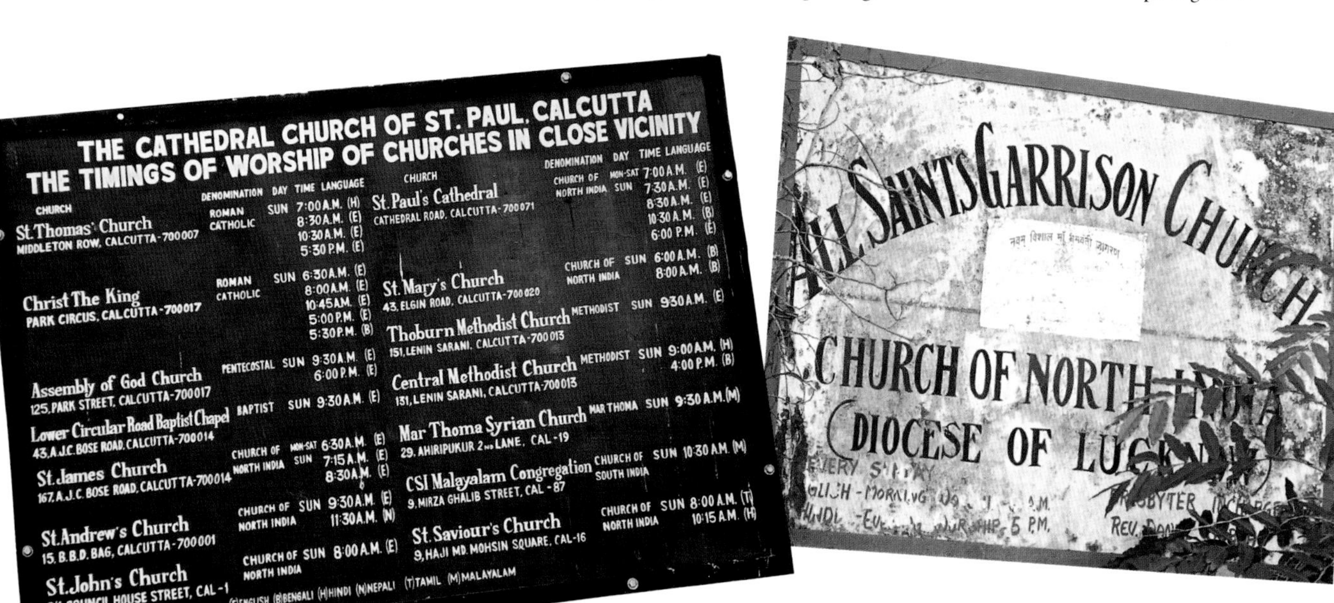

BELOW LEFT Signboard outside St Paul's Cathedral, Calcutta. Consecrated in 1847, the design was based on that of Norwich Cathedral. A stained glass window by Burne Jones overlooks the west portico.

BELOW RIGHT Signboard outside All Saints Garrison Church, Lucknow, an enormous disused red brick Victorian Church.

RIGHT The Cathedral at Thiruvananthapurum – more pronounceably – Trivandrum – rises out of the Keralan palm groves.

INDIAN
GEO PLAST
ALPHA KURIES
ARCHANA ELECTRONICS

of the Company school were never architects by profession, but by happenstance; if a church was required, it usually fell into the hands of the engineers to produce one. The delightful church opposite the club in Cochin Fort, all Anglican cosiness and virtue, was converted from a former Dutch church – part of the English movement to replace Dutch churches in their former trading enclave.

The Company's own chapel in Poplar High Street, one of the few to be built during Cromwell's Commonwealth, was innovative and influential in design. However, it was only adopted as a model by the church builders of the American colonies. It was not until Gibbs created his masterpiece of St Martin's-in-the-Fields that a paradigm of classical elegance was created which could be simply emulated in the colonies, with added local touches. Gibbs's church, completed in 1726, was widely imitated in America, and echoes of it crop up in India such as St John's in Calcutta, Bombay, Poona, Madras and Meerut; its popularity lasted through most of the Gothic revival back home. The English architectural style remained resolutely classical in India until mid-Victorian times; porticoes and colonnades seemed somehow in tune with the spirit of Empire, both through the conscious emulation of the glories of Greece and Rome and an

BELOW **St John's, Calcutta, consecrated in 1787; the main church until St Paul's '. . . claimed India as the Lord's'.**

ABOVE St James' Church, Old Delhi. Built by the Anglo-Indian Captain James Skinner, supposedly to fulfil a promise.

appreciation of its suitability to the climate. Gibbs's design chimed harmoniously with that spirit, and the curious sensation of looking at a familiar London scene when admiring a print of many English towns in India is partly down to its influence.

If the history of the British in India is written in their buildings, there is no more eloquent testament to this than St James's church in Delhi. It was built by Colonel James Skinner, the pre-eminent Anglo-Indian hero who was the son of a Scotsman descended from the Provost of Montrose, and the daughter of a Rajput zamindar. He was raised a Christian but was barred, by a general decree excluding Anglo-Indians in 1792, from joining the Company's service. As a result, he founded an irregular troop of cavalry known as Skinner's Horse, which enjoyed a spectacular and adventurous career in north-west India as a mercenary outfit in the service of various Mahratta potentates. The inspiration for his church supposedly came when his corps was hired to fight the Rajah of Ooneara by the Rajah of Karowlee. Beset by treachery, he relates that he was wounded in the groin on the field near Tonke. Insensible the first night, the second he spent listening to the jackals eating the dead on the battlefield. Morning conjured up an old low-caste woman who gave him bread and water, a succour which prompted his vow 'if he should ultimately be preserved, and ever have the means, to build a Christian Church'. This showed extraordinary, if not downright fanciful, prescience, as twenty-five years later he did indeed have the considerable means (£20,000) required.

In the meantime, he had been grudgingly admitted to the Company's ranks. Skinner ran his cavalry in an unorthodox way, one innovation being the introduction of the durbar, or council, at which any of his soldiers could raise problems with senior officers. An adaptation of a Moghul tradition, the durbar gave Skinner an intimacy with his troops that in turn enhanced their own prestige. Skinner fathered a substantial Anglo-Indian dynasty: according to his family he had seven wives, and according to legend, fourteen. He certainly built a mosque for a Muslim one and a temple for a Hindu one before getting around to his promise of creating a proper Christian church. Eighty children claimed him as their father, although his fame was such that considerable advantage might have attached thereto.

Rumoured to have been designed by Skinner himself, his church was consecrated in 1836, and even before that the first to be buried there was his great friend William Fraser, who was assassinated in 1835. Eventually, Skinner was laid to rest alongside him in 1841. The Church is close to Fraser's own house and the Residency, in the quarter of Old Delhi near the Kashmir Gate, scene of great dramas in the Mutiny. The richness of the history is maintained today; Skinner's Horse is still a regiment in the Indian Army, an annual thanksgiving ceremony is held in St James's; and a descendant of Skinner leads the restoration appeal. Skinner's Horse received the President's Standard in 1971, with the vicar of St James's taking part in the ceremony. Although he suffered prejudice because of it in his own lifetime, it is the Anglo-Indian aspect of his story that has given it a tangible continuity through to the present.

The missionaries, and the evangelical zeal that accompanied them, brought to India a new architectural style for churches, and a new scale of operation. Bombay already had a cathedral; there had been a gradual accretion on the fabric of the garrison church, and Madras sported a vast Gibbsian structure. Calcutta had a bishop but no cathedral but entered the lists in style. No longer content simply to serve the needs of the English, the Gothic churches and cathedrals of the high Victorian age needed to proclaim Christ from the very steeple tops. In his address for the dedication of St Paul's Cathedral in Calcutta in 1847, Bishop Wilson said of the building that 'it claims India as the Lord's', and in its overblown and clumsy Gothic styling, it was an unequivocal statement of the particular brand of spiritual power that the English now

OPPOSITE **St Thomas' Cathedral, Bombay. Based on an eighteenth century church, it had accreted sufficient spiritual gravitas by 1883 to be made a cathedral.**

PSALMS

desired to foist on the subcontinent. It reached its architectural apogee with Lahore Cathedral, the spiritual phalanx of the 'Forward Policy' which had annexed the Punjab and subdued the Frontier. The fact that the Sikhs and Muslims failed to convert in droves must have puzzled the first bishop, Thomas French, who had been promoted from the ranks of missionaries.

High latitude encouraged more modest effusions. The hill stations of India were the highest expression of the English desire for a home-from-home, and as the earliest of them became properly fashionable only after the Mutiny, their churches are mostly in the Gothic style, and contribute enormously to the pervading sense of English 'villageness'.

The new style also commemorated their greatest of follies. The Afghan Church in Bombay was built as a memorial to the First Afghan War, and the officers who perished there. It is oddly touching to see the name of Alexander Burnes, a participant of the Great Game, who had been hacked to pieces in Kabul bazaar, inscribed on the wall of such a quintessentially peaceful English church. Most of the men listed perished in the icebound retreat from Kabul, a catastrophe that exploded the myth of British supremacy in the subcontinent. Outside the church, the birds swoop amongst the eucalyptus trees and a marriage bureau has set up stall against the railings. Thus great events of history and the great events in human lives are brought together in the dappled sunlight.

LEFT Christ Church, Simla, consecrated in 1857. One vicar complained from the pulpit that all the space was taken up by the women's crinolines. The next week they all attended in their riding habits.

RIGHT The Afghan Church, Bombay, consecrated in 1865. A fine Gothic Revival monument to that monumental folly, the First Afghan War.

Graveyards

In St Giles Cathedral, Edinburgh, there is a memorial to the 488 soldiers, 47 wives and 124 children of the 78th Highlanders who died of cholera on the banks of the Indus during the winter of 1844–45. From start to end the most valuable export from Britain to the Raj was the lives of its citizens who succumbed to war, disease, alcohol and wildlife in prodigious quantities. Two monsoons was supposed to be the life expectancy of a Company servant in the early years, and much of the considerable wealth amassed by these merchants was acquired at great personal risk. For every nabob returning to England to buy up a rotten borough and a country estate there were a dozen forgotten aspirants buried in that far-off soil. The Reverend Ovington wrote about the English Graveyard at Surat as early as 1690: 'They endeavour to outvie each other in magnificent Structures and stately Monuments, whose large Extent, beautiful Architecture, and aspiring Heads, make them visible at a remote distance, lovely Objects of the sight, and give them the title of the Principal Ornaments and Magnificences about the City.'

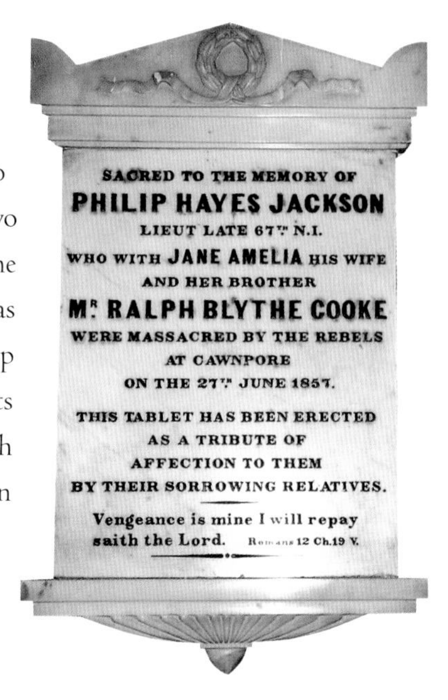

ABOVE A tablet on the wall of All Soul's Memorial Church at Cawnpore, now Kanpur. The restrained inscription belies the savagery of the event.

LEFT Raymond's tomb at Hyderabad. An Englishman, he rose from the ranks of the Nizam's army to earn the command of 15,000 troops and the combined Hindu-Muslim name of Moosa Ram.

ABOVE The ashes of generations of Hindu dead have whirled slowly by the British cemetery at Chunar on the holy Ganges.

The graveyards of India have a particular poignancy for the British. They resemble, albeit on a generally grander scale, familiar graveyards back home, and so beg the question 'What are these people doing here?', unmourned and so far from their roots. What they were doing, of course, was building an Empire, and the neglect of their graves marks that Empire's decline. The inscriptions often tell distinctively subcontinental tales, of battles won, mutinies quelled and railways built; or of tragic losses of the young to snake bites or malaria.

PREVIOUS PAGE **Necropolis becomes metropolis. The living and the dead live harmoniously in Park Street Cemetery, Calcutta.**

OPPOSITE **The Victoria Memorial, Calcutta. A museum dedicated to the history of the British in India in one of the Raj's more spectacular buildings.**

The British Association for Cemeteries in South Asia, a London-based charitable concern, tries to look after the graveyards, but the imperatives of India frequently overwhelm their efforts. The massive tombs of the larger cemeteries serve as accommodation for the otherwise homeless, and the dead and the living make excellent bedfellows. The British themselves set a precedent for this, occasionally coopting the great mausoleums of their predecessors, the Moghuls, to make an impromptu residency, such as at Lahore, which occupied the tomb of Mohammed Kasim Khan, a cousin of Akbar the Great. The gift of cultural absorption seems to be the inheritance of the very soil of India, and as empires and warring kingdoms play out their dramas on its landscape, the strata of history gradually accumulate and the remains of each is absorbed by the next. India is never really conquered, it merely serves as temporary accommodation for sundry dynastic ambitions, whilst the epochs unravel.

The most touching graves can be found far from consecrated ground, such as in the remote districts of the North West Frontier. A young woman, perhaps taken off by cholera, buried in the grounds of the District Commissioner's bungalow like a much-loved pet. No weeping angels mark her passing, nor high-flown sentiments, but a simple gravestone. Quiet dignity marks the grave of one the Empire's most honoured servants, Sir Henry Lawrence, who died at the Siege of Lucknow. At his own request his monument bears the most English of inscriptions: 'Here lies Sir Henry Lawrence who tried to do his duty. May God have mercy on him.' It would make an apt epitaph for the Raj itself.

There are graveyards for the memorials of India as well. The statues that used to ennoble the vistas in the big towns and cities – from the ubiquitous Victoria memorials to obscure generals killed in long-forgotten actions – but failed to maintain their position in the post-Partition status quo, have fled en masse to remoter parks and gardens to forgather and reminisce. However, with so much virtue and duty on display they must make for dull company. Does Sir John Lawrence still seek to explain to his Queen the finer points of 'Masterful Inactivity', and Lord Dalhousie defend his 'Doctrine of Lapse'? Or do they ponder the significance of the upstart statues that have usurped their rightful places, the Shivajis and Gandhis? Does George V, surveying Coronation Park outside Delhi from atop his fifty-foot pedestal, resent the fact that he no longer occupies the prime position in Kingsway, the greatest ceremonial avenue in the new capital he commissioned?

RIGHT The Residency, Lucknow. Scene of one of the most remarkable sieges of history in 1857, when 3,000 British residents and loyal Indian troops took refuge here under the command of Sir Henry Lawrence. This is the principal building, from the shattered tower of which a Union Jack was kept defiantly flying until Independence.

BELOW The view from the tower. The siege lasted from June to October during the hot season; the Residency was then relieved and promptly besieged again until the final relief on November 17th.

LEFT The Banqueting Hall was separate from the main building, and was used as a hospital during the siege. The brother of the ex-King of Oudh was kept prisoner here, which constrained the besiegers' fire.

BELOW Gubbins' Battery was an outwork which protected the south-west corner of the Residency and was garrisoned by civilians from Mr Gubbins' House nearby. Gubbins, the Financial Secretary of Oudh, was renowned, and resented, for the quality of his table even at the height of the siege.

FAR LEFT Cawnpore, now Kanpur. A view of the Ganges from the steps at Sati Chaura Ghat on which the initial massacre took place. The British had been promised a safe passage by boat to Allahabad when Nana Sahib's troops opened fire, and took the women and children captive.

LEFT The Mutiny Memorial which used to stand over the well into which the bodies of women and children were thrown. The statue is by Carlo Marachetti; Queen Victoria later commissioned him to sculpt a memorial to Albert at Windsor. The screen was designed by Henry Yule, who also co-wrote 'Hobson-Jobson', the classic Anglo-Indian dictionary.

On one issue they would be unanimous. The Cawnpore Memorial was at one time the *sanctum sanctorum* of the Indian Empire: 'Remember Cawnpore! Remember the Ladies!' was the cry on every vengeful soldier's lips as he slaughtered mutineers and innocents alike. The hideous Cawnpore massacre was recalled by an Angel of the Resurrection poised over the filled-in well that had contained the bodies of the women and children slaughtered in the Bibigurh, a house built by an English officer for the accommodation of his Indian mistresses. The Angel has since flown to the rear of the memorial church, leaving the well unguarded in the memorial gardens, now renamed Nana Rao Park, after the perpetrator of the massacre. One can almost see the outrage on the noble sculpted brows.

Museums & Heritage

The attitude of the English to the monuments of their predecessors on the subcontinent was mixed. Those with an interest in oriental culture were fascinated by the pristine purity of Moghul architecture and the organic strangeness of many Hindu buildings. Others thought them merely alien and ugly, but thankfully the English did not, as was once suggested, demolish the Taj Mahal for its marble. With characteristic thoroughness they recorded in meticulous detail many of the more spectacular monuments, initially through drawings and later by photography. The curiosity concerning landscape and architecture of those who had never been to India was catered for by the artists who started to make careers there from the late eighteenth century onwards. Thomas and William Daniell, George Chinnery, Zoffany and many others, professional and amateur alike, portrayed the Indian scene, revealing its richness and variety of culture.

However, the English maintained their control over the land by force, and that sometimes caused, perforce, the destruction of monuments. Nineteenth-century reinforcements of Akbar's fort at Allahabad, founded in 1583, required the demolition of the 'Forty Pillared Hall', an unique three-storeyed octagonal marble pavilion overlooking the river. Revenge drove the British to raze the magnificent Nawab's palace at Lucknow after the Mutiny. In an act of cultural vandalism on a scale similar to the destruction of the Summer Palace at Peking, the interior of the Red Fort at Delhi was stripped of all its Moghul gardens and courtyards, stranding the sublime Pearl Mosque, the Diwan-i-am and other exquisite pavilions in a sea of featureless lawns, tastefully enhanced by a British barracks of peculiar ugliness.

LEFT The Red Fort, Delhi. From the neatly-trimmed lawns which replaced the Moghul gardens, ponds and courtyards that the English destroyed, looking towards the Naqqar Khana, the 'House of Drums'.

OPPOSITE The Red Fort, Delhi. The Pearl Mosque, happily spared the ravages of the vengeful English.

They could be equally over-zealous in their more constructive efforts. In the case of the Dance Hall in the Palace of Madurai, the restoration included the addition of plaster decorations reminiscent of the nearby temple, and Curzon caused the minarets of the gate to Akbar's Tomb at Sikandra to be finished off. As Viceroy at the beginning of the last century, Curzon initiated a renewed interest in the preservation of India's architectural heritage, being appalled to find that 'historic fabrics of a bygone age' were 'tumbling into irretrievable ruin, all for the want of a directing hand and a few thousand rupees'. He had spent much time in his youth at the British Museum studying ancient sculpture, and had acquired considerable expertise, so that when he set up the Archaeological Survey of India, he was able plausibly to appoint himself Director of Antiquities. He ploughed some of his personal fortune – or, more accurately, the fortune of his personable American heiress wife, Mary – into the restoration of monuments and, as well as carrying out vital work on the structure, redesigned the gardens of the Taj Mahal, thus having a hand in both saving and framing the world's most famous view. He visited the major monuments himself, inspecting and authorising expenditure. Ruins such as the gate of the ancient city of Gour, former capital of the sixteenth-century rulers of Bengal, were saved from dereliction, and the structure was restored. This work receives scant recognition from visitors to the heritage sites in India today, but the conservation-minded British saved much that would otherwise have been ruined. The Survey continues its work still, notoriously underfunded; recent legislation allowing sites to charge foreign tourists significantly more may do something to alleviate the decay of the monuments, to which India's increasingly vicious air pollution has added significantly.

LEFT **The Residency at Hyderabad, built for Colonel James Kirkpatrick by the obliging Nizam. It is now the University College for Women.**

The British also restored India to its rightful place in the pantheon of the ancient world. The discovery of Harappa and Mohenjo Daro, and Sir Mortimer Wheeler's subsequent excavations of them during the 1920s and 1930s, established that the Indus Valley civilisation was contemporary to, and as significant as the ancient civilisations of Egypt and Mesopotamia. Eschewing the spectacular temples and palaces of the others, the Indus civilisation had remained unknown until the chance discovery of Mohenjo Daro as a railway line was being laid in Sind. It has since been established that it was a sophisticated network of small cities within a well-ordered political and social structure. At its height this culture covered a larger area than either of its more celebrated rivals, and although its script remains undeciphered, recent research suggests that it may predate the earliest known human writing, the cuneiform of Mesopotamia. Sir Aurel Stein revealed the full extent of the Graeco-Buddhist Gandharan culture, which straddled north-west India and Afghanistan from before the time of Christ, and fought against the desecration of Buddhist sculptures and cave paintings on the Silk Route by Muslim inhabitants. A similar situation persists in latter-day Afghanistan where the vast, magnificent Buddhist statues and cave paintings at Bamian have been blown up by local Taliban commanders; and the Gandharan treasures of the Kabul Museum, regarded as pre-Islamic and thus idolatrous, have been packed in wooden cases and sent off to undisclosed locations, much to the horror of the art world.

LEFT Mohenjo Daro, the 'City of the Dead', one of the principal cities of the previously unknown ancient Indus Valley civilisation which was discovered by the British at the beginning of the twentieth century.

ABOVE Brick walls at Mohenjo Daro. Only the eighth century Buddhist stupa was visible before the ancient city's discovery beneath.

Although some of the wealth of art and antiquities discovered in India found their way back to Britain (the Victoria and Albert Museum being the principal beneficiary, inheriting the bulk of the *ad hoc* museum that had formed at East India House), the administration in India had the foresight to establish museums in India itself. The happy result is that many of the subcontinent's finest artefacts have been preserved, properly housed and displayed. It would be no exaggeration to say that the British preserved for posterity a vast amount of the artistic heritage of India, which might otherwise have been broken up for building materials, burnt to produce lime or otherwise destroyed. It is one of the great and most lasting achievements of the Raj. The first such institution was the Indian Museum in Calcutta, which opened in 1875. It grew from the activities of the Asia Society, and houses mineralogical and botanical collections, as well as a collection of second-century BC Buddhist sculptures saved from destruction by General Alexander Cunningham in 1873. The Prince of Wales Museum in Bombay and the State Museum in Madras followed; the latter contains the Amaravati Collection, the remaining sculptures from a ruined Buddhist stupa which were rescued by an Englishman, Colonel Colin Mackenzie. Curzon commissioned the Victoria Memorial Museum which was the Raj's splendid memorial to itself, containing material relating to colonial times in India. He called it 'a sort of valhalla of (British) Indian heroes and worthies with the Queen at the centre'. The Lahore Museum, or the 'Wonder House' immortalised in the opening chapter of Kipling's *Kim,* contains the subcontinent's finest collection of Gandharan sculpture. Curzon also initiated 'site museums' run by the Archaeological Survey on important sites such as Agra and Sanchi. There are now thirty-three such museums in India. Whilst there is a more than a hint of Imperial complacency in the suggestion that the British directly and indirectly saved Indian heritage for (and from) the Indians, there would appear to be considerable evidence in support of the notion.

This contribution of the British to the preservation of the cultural heritage of India led to a wider appreciation of Indian art amongst the Indians themselves, with the result that since Independence a number of new museums have been set up, often by private individuals. The Textile Museum at Ahmadabad is one of the most successful examples, founded in 1949 through the enthusiasm of Ms. Gira Sarabhai. Many of the endangered textile techniques of India have enjoyed a resurgence as a result of its activities.

RIGHT **Peshawar Museum, which houses a fine collection of Gandharan Buddhist sculptures.**

PESHAWAR MUSEUM

V

INFRASTRUCTURE

East meets West:
the redoubtable elephant of
India confronts the inevitability
of the iron horse. A panel
on the facade of Victoria
Station, Bombay.

Railways, Bridges & Roads

The Roman Empire ran on roads, and the Raj ran on rails. The single biggest contribution made by the British to the subcontinent, and their most enduring memorial, is the Indian railway system. Superficially, nothing more captures the essence of residual Englishness in India than its railways; the steam engines, the stations, the waiting rooms, the porters, the station masters, the bridges, the tunnels – the whole ensemble seems to derive from a golden British railway age, and remains a subject of fascination. Train enthusiasts will travel halfway across the world to take the narrow-gauge lines to Simla or Darjeeling. The Frontier Mail sounds as romantic today as it did when it was first built, despite the fact that it now runs only as far as the frontier with Pakistan at Firozpor, rather than all the way to Peshawar. What could be a more apt railway cathedral than the Victoria Terminus in Bombay? It is the largest nineteenth-century building in Asia – 'too good for the natives', pronounced Lady Dufferin, the presiding Vicerene, when it opened in 1889.

Not only is the railway system the fourth largest in the world, it has continued to expand since Independence, unlike its counterparts in developed countries. The railways are the country's largest employer with nearly two million full-time staff. They carry four billion passengers a year and three hundred million tonnes of freight. Trains have been manufactured in India since 1895, and some have been bought from Sweden, Austria, Hungary and Canada, and they use tracks on technology from Japan, Italy, Switzerland and France. Indian railway engineering prowess has been deployed abroad for many years; the infamous man-eating lions of Tsavo dined on Indian indentured labourers building the Mombasa to Nairobi line in the 1890s, and Indian engineers successfully constructed a high-speed railway in Iraq. As befits an enterprise on this scale, Indian railways are thoroughly international, and although the roots of the system lie in the fertile soil of the Empire, like the banyan tree it now spreads its offshoots far beyond the field of its original conception. As Oswald Nock, the rail historian, commented, 'after Independence the transfer of railway stocks amounted to one of the most phenomenal take-overs in transport history with regard to the smooth assumption of power, both administrative and technical, by Indian staff.'

RIGHT **The Darjeeling narrow-gauge railway still uses steam locomotives.**

85

By contrast, the railways of Pakistan are far less evolved, principally because the region was a late-comer to the British fold, and because these railways were built primarily for strategic purposes. The lines to the Khyber Pass and across Baluchistan to Zaidan in Iran enabled troops to be deployed with greater rapidity on the fragile frontiers of the Empire, but they were not designed specifically to serve the civilian population. A subsequent lack of investment has meant that the system mainly runs on lines established by its British forbear, and frequently with trains built by them. Bangladesh's 2,700km of British-built railway lines have scarcely expanded, principally because of the cost, as well as the technical problems of building railways in a country criss-crossed by rivers and beset by floods. Whilst the railways of both these countries are by default closer to the original British scheme they inherited at Partition, they are but handmaidens to the glories that are the present-day Indian railways.

ABOVE Lahore, Pakistan. The railway station which witnessed the dreadful consequences of the Partition atrocities.

RIGHT The Raja Hodi tunnel nearing completion in 1883. The subcontinent tested Victorian engineering skills, but the Queen believed 'We are capable of anything'.

1883
RAJA HODI

The subcontinent's railway system always seemed to be an expression in iron and steam of the Imperial impulse, ruthless pragmatism allied to evangelical zeal. What better example could there be of the 'straight and narrow' than a railway line across the Deccan plain, bringing enlightenment to the previously inaccessible heathen soul? What great benevolence and usefulness lay behind the mighty exertions necessary to burrow railways under mountain ranges, or throw them across tiger-infested gorges and swirling rivers? How noble was the sacrifice of four thousand labourers' lives to breach the Ghats? And what man more appropriate to champion the cause of railways than the Governor-General Dalhousie himself? As a former President of the Board of Trade in England, he knew his railways better than most, and, in particular, managed to avoid the one glaring problem that had bedevilled the development of the railways back home: disputes about gauge. In a manner that could only have emanated from his Olympian position, Dalhousie decreed that Indian railways should have a 5ft 6in broad gauge, which remains his most important legacy. His proposal lasted nineteen years, until Lord Mayo's disastrous diversification into the metre gauge in 1872. Metre-gauge lines were envisaged as feeder lines for the broad-gauge system but are almost invariably loss-making as they are unable to carry the volumes of freight and passenger traffic that would make them cost-effective. As picturesque as they frequently are, the narrow-gauge lines employed for hill stations and some of the princely states are heavily dependent on tourists and train enthusiasts for their viability.

Matters of gauge should not be dismissed as only of technical interest. When heroines in south Indian films are required to commit suicide by throwing themselves in front of a train, they inevitably prefer the broad gauge (although in the films of the north, jumping off the Lakshman Jula Bridge at Rishikesh is considered a more picturesque exit). Also, there are opponents of Hindu Nationalism who regard the broad gauge with intense suspicion as it is most intensively used in the Gangetic basin, in the Hindi heartland.

Dalhousie dreamt up the great Indian railway initiative in his mountain retreat. In a carefully-argued fifty-page document of May 1850, he posited 'the three great engines of social improvement – railways, uniform postage and the electric telegraph'. Plans had been mooted for railways in India from 1832, but first off the buffers was the Great Indian Peninsular Railway Company's Bombay–Thana line, officially opened in 1853. By 1869 over 4,000 miles of track lay across the land and by 1906, 30,000 miles had been laid, with the railways' strategic and economic importance to the Empire never in question. This was the case after the Mutiny, when some stations and bridges took on the appearance of fortresses in an attempt to avoid that catastrophe again. In 1926, in the unruly North West Frontier, the designs for the Khyber signal called for 'Combined Booking Office Window and Machine Gun Loophole'.

ABOVE **Higginbothams book-stall on the platform of Ootacamund station.**

As an engine of Empire, the railways were singularly successful, providing ready access to markets, swift troop transportation, mobility of the workforce and a drive for political unity. Gandhi condemned them in his *Hindu Swaraj* of 1908: 'Railways accentuate the evil nature of man. Bad men fulfil their evil designs with greater rapidity . . .' In any case, the political designs of the rapidly growing Congress were enormously assisted by the rail system, and Gandhi himself made full use of it to take his message to the people. As much as the English language provided a common basis for law and administration, the railways conferred a new physical unity upon the subcontinent. The journey from Delhi to Calcutta now took only several days as opposed to the seven months in the early days of the nineteenth century. Ironically, Gandhi's stated opposition to rail may have come from the experience he had of being detrained on racial grounds in South Africa in 1893 for ignoring the convention of hiring sheets in first-class sleepers.

Trains were the engine of both liberty and of death in the terrible aftermath of Partition; descriptions of refugee trains drawing into Lahore and Amritsar to reveal nothing more than carriage after carriage of corpses, and station platforms acting as temporary morgues haunt the history of that time. Trains mobilised the fugitive population, but were easy prey to those who sought bloody reprisals. As we have seen with many aspects of the Raj, the things that facilitated the Empire's supremacy also contained the seeds of its destruction, and in no case is this more brutally apparent than in the ghastly service performed by the trains of the Punjab in the implementation of Partition.

But, as we ride the Empire Express out of the dark tunnel of despond into the bright sunlight of the plains, what can we still discern of their British heritage in the swash and buckle of the railroads across the land? There are stations aplenty – some 7,000 are now in existence. There are 42,000 level crossings and every one is manned. Of the 100,000 bridges, 10,000 are reckoned to be of a major size. The vast lakes of carefully monitored and up dated statistics dryly relate the story of what is the second biggest enterprise on earth (although on what statistical basis this claim is made is not clear, nor which is the biggest . . .). These statistics are faithfully churned out of Rail Bhavan in New Delhi, the Indian Railways British-built headquarters, said to be the cleanest, most orderly office building in India.

A trawl through the figures reveals that 75 per cent of the railways' revenues come from goods trains, each carrying 1,000 tonnes of freight at an average speed of 23kph. There are 350,000 freight cars in India. Broad-gauge trains account for 90 per cent of freight, and 82 per cent of passenger revenues. Each train involves the direct or indirect efforts of 1,000 people. Indian Railways houses 37 per cent of its employees, operates 750 educational establishments, runs 100 hospitals and has 50,000 medical staff. The line to Bardapur has 581 bridges over a distance of 162km. The highest broad-gauge line in the world is 997m, atop the Eastern Ghats at Bastar in south India. Venkatanarasingharaluvariapeta near Turapti is the longest station name in India; the longest platform 833m is at Kharagpur. The last steam engine built in India was in 1972. The largest number of locomotives built in one class is 2,450. The oldest working steam engine in India, the Tweed, was built in 1873. The 'calculated fare table' details passenger luggage allowances, including three small calves under 0.76m and snakes in baskets 'securely fastened with close fitting lids'.

Above left A sign outside the ticket office on the Kalka-Simla narrow-gauge line. Note the Orwellian slogan.

Left The station sign on the Kalka-Simla narrow-gauge railway carries distinct echoes of the London Underground.

The vast amount of statistics are not a recent addition to the complexities of the railway system; they were gathered from the start, and not always accurately. East India Railways claimed that in the first six months of 1897 they had carried '26,328 elephants and one sheep' until the mistake was rectified. Nor were statistics necessarily practically applied; when the third-class

ABOVE Old Delhi station, built in the best post-Mutiny semi-fortified style.

carriages on the Oudh Rohikand railways were fitted with toilets, '. . . the hole in the floor was only five inches – apparently the designer had taken a first-class closet as his standard, and made the diameter of the orifice in proportion to the fare'. Despite this aberration, India was generally well ahead of the West in providing bathroom facilities on trains.

It is no coincidence that the golden age of the railways occurred at the height of the British Imperial ambitions. The force of steam unleashed by the Industrial Revolution had many consequences directly connected with Britain's ability to forge an Empire, and none more so than the possibilities opened up by the iron road. In England, what is still considered historically as the best and safest railway gauge, Brunel's seven-foot gauge (Firefly, the locomotive class for this gauge, capable even then of a safe ninety miles per hour, is dazzlingly caught by Turner's painting 'Rain, Steam and Speed' at the Tate Gallery in London), had disappeared in a heap of invective and vested interest by the end of the century. Had the gauge survived as the standard, instead of the 4ft 8" standard, the current state of the UK's rail freight industry might be remarkably different. Drawing on his understanding of the virtues of Brunel's gauge but recognising its high cost, the compromise of the broad gauge set up by Dalhousie in India was a stroke of genius. The economic consequences are still possible to discern in that pool of statistics as it is possible to divine the failure of Mayo's miserable metre gauge, which started its life of servitude inauspiciously in 1841 in a Derbyshire lime quarry, where many feel it should have remained.

In the soul-searching climate that is the aftermath of privatisation, comparisons between the state of Indian railways today as opposed to those of the land that spawned them are inevitable. The notice to workers on South Central Railways that 'The only effective safety device is a careful employee', has particular resonance for those who daily place their lives in the hands of the notoriously unreliable Railtrack and its motley crew of subcontractors. Indian railways still rehearse and enforce strict safety procedures to deal with the landslides, bridge collapses, flooding and other such disasters that are part of daily life on the tempestuous subcontinent. When the East India Company first reported to Parliament in 1845 regarding the potential for railways in India, they laid great emphasis on the problems that might arise from climate and in particular 'the influence of a vertical sun and . . . spontaneous vegetation' (an early variant, perhaps, of 'leaves on the line') and even Dalhousie considered that the issue of cows straying on to the lines required 'desperate nostrums'. The technical problems that had to be surmounted to bring rail transport to India were enormous, and the fact that they continue to be surmounted is a matter of pride in their technical prowess for Indian engineers. When a tidal wave washed away the 107 spans of the Pamban railway bridge to Rameshwaram in 1964, the whole thing was up and running again within nine weeks; it is inconceivable that a similar feat could be accomplished in Britain today.

LEFT A miniature Clifton suspension bridge spans the Ramganga River in the Corbett National Park tiger reserve. It is rumoured to have been built to plans sent out to India by Isambard Kingdom Brunel.

Manpower is of course a significant contributor to this ability to respond quickly and effectively; however, national ownership, employee pride and a supportive Government all help immeasurably. There are two principal concerns for observers of Indian railways at present: firstly, that the increasing temperature in the communal and caste debates, largely as a result of resurgent Hindu Nationalism, will increase pressure on the fragile national unity of which the railways are the most conspicuously functioning example. Secondly, that the chill wind of free market economics will compel the Government to look at the railways in the same way they have at the airlines. One can imagine what privatisation, a disaster in Britain, would cause in India. 'A government always works at greater expense than anybody else,' Dalhousie opined. That, however, didn't prevent him from using his Government's money to underwrite the private capital raised to build railways for the greater good of the country. Later, most expenditure on railways was paid for entirely by the Government.

The Victorians certainly knew how to build to last. Short-termism was an alien concept to a nation fully anticipating remaining at the helm of planetary affairs for the foreseeable future. Were it not for their almost pathological over-specification, the great Victorian infrastructure projects in Britain would have collapsed long ago and the country's covert attempt to join the Third World would have been more successful. The brooding stone dams of the Pennines retain reservoirs that still largely provide the needs of the northern cities, and Victorian bridges, tunnels and cuttings provide the basis of the railway system, even if the trains frequently resemble buses with the tyres left off. In Britain, labour for these enterprises was largely provided by migrant Irish navvies who had grown accustomed to hewing huge quantities of stone and digging up vast swathes of country from the canal era, which could be thought of as a warm-up exercise for the railways. In India, the equivalent of the navvies were the coolies, a name derived, as Hobson-Jobson puts it, 'from a race or caste . . . whose savagery, filth and general degradation attracted much attention in former times'. The fact that they died in their tens of thousands during the building of the railways, however, failed to attract much attention at all. The image of the colonial engineer, braving the hazards of heat, disease and wildlife to drive the railways through a hostile land, fails to take into account the fact that when he retired to his tent at the end of a hard day his workforce might be considerably lighter than when he got up. It was ever thus: the name Brunel resounds through the ages, whilst who remembers the name of a single navvy?

These forced sacrifices created a system that is still a wonder of the world, 'a series of public monuments vastly surpassing, in real grandeur, the aqueducts of Rome, the pyramids of Egypt, the great wall of China', as the engineer W. P. Andrews wrote in 1946 when the Indian railways were just a twinkle in Dalhousie's eye – you can rarely beat a Victorian empire builder for sheer

अवकाश गृह
HOLIDAY HOME
CULTURAL UNIT
WELCOME TO
DARJEELING
WBY 2532
WBY 380

magnitude of vision. The railways in India were the product of an age when all seemed possible, and seeming so, became so. In 1851 the Queen wrote in her diary: 'We are capable of doing anything.'

With steam largely a thing of the past, some of the charm has inevitably disappeared from the Indian railways. Although the views from a carriage on the Simla line are spectacular, they somehow seem less so when pulled by a diesel engine. However steam is still the power behind the locomotives of many other narrow-gauge lines, and the train to Darjeeling is well-known to tourists and rail enthusiasts alike. There are other eccentricities in the railway system to be admired. The line to Ootacamund incorporates Swiss track technology; the 116km Bamboo line to Haflong in Assam ends with a ride to town in a bus which has a thatched roof. Dabhoi in Gujerat is the hub of five little lines, each installed by a separate Princely State – the rulers of these, by and large, were the prime movers behind the narrow-gauge movement – not feeling compelled to submit to the British broad- and meter-gauge dictats. Initially regarding railways with a degree of hauteur, placing stations a disdainful distance from their homes, the Maharajahs and Nizams eventually succumbed to their charms: Scindia of Gwalior built a line right to his palace gate.

LEFT The busy rail station in the hill station of Darjeeling.

BELOW A Darjeeling narrow-gauge line steam locomotive.

RIGHT Echoes of the glory that was Rome. A spectacular bridge on the Simla line.

RIGHT Howrah Bridge, Calcutta. One of the busiest – and ugliest – bridges in the world.

For those with an interest in British-built railway tunnels and bridges – a branch of train-spotting, but without the attendant danger of the object of affection departing unexpectedly – India presents a host of delights for even the most jaded of engineering palates. Bridges in the manner of Roman aqueducts sustain the Simla line, whereas elsewhere the rails are more delicately poised on wooden stilts. Ungainly, but eminently practical iron monstrosities span the great rivers – the Howrah across the Hughli, the double-decker Attock bridge across the Indus in the shadow of Akbar's Fort (sadly now superseded by a new one), the Landsdowne at Sukkur and the bridge over the Sarabati River at Ahmedabad, built from sections sent out by Braithwaite and Kirk of West Bromwich in 1887. Devotees of the art of tunnelling will again find satisfaction on the Simla line, although the longest in India is the Khojak tunnel on the Chaman Extension Railway which steams right up to the Afghan frontier. It was built in the 1880s to counter the ever-present-if-never-manifest Russian threat, and thus forms a fitting 12,780-feet-long monument to the Great Game.

Those passengers who are tired of the scenery on Indian railways can always call at a station book store before setting off. Like W. H. Smith's, founded at Euston by a clergyman manqué, railway bookshops were often set up with the intention of providing improving literature for the traveller, but they now mainly deal the standard international fare of blockbusters and magazines. North India bookworms have been fed for over a century by A. H. Wheeler of Allahabad which has shops at 264 stations, whereas south India has the rival Higginbothams'. A less spiritual fare is provided by the hundreds of food vendors and chai wallahs who service the trains from the platform, providing cheap, freshly-made food and tea to the passengers through the windows. A true reflection of the one-nation effect of the railways can be seen in the increasing popularity of rumali rotis in the south and dhosas and idlis in the north.

LEFT A platform buffet trolley on Lahore Station, Pakistan. Food and drink supplies are an integral feature of subcontinental train culture.

The apotheosis of the Indian railway system, indeed of that of the whole world, is the cathedral of steam Victoria Terminus in Bombay. The elegant grandeur of Paddington, the vaulting space of Grand Central Station, and the flamboyance of St Pancras are left standing by the sheer scale and exuberance of VT. Two and a half million people pass through it every day, pushing, pulling, sitting, shouting, praying, lying, sleeping, eating, even cooking within its protective embrace, and somehow it still manages to fulfil its original function. Unusually for the Raj, VT was built by a practising architect F. W. Stevens, and opened in 1887. Bedecked like a Hindu idol with a mishmash of grotesque sculpted animals, with railway symbols that seem to hint at some arcane art, and saintly portraits of the Queen-Empress and her angelic host (the Viceroy down to the Chief Engineer of the Great Indian Peninsula Railway), VT's exterior has a peculiar cocktail of styles known in *Murray's Handbook to India* as 'Italian-Gothic, with certain Oriental modifications in the domes'. However strange the recipe, the result is staggering in scale (both large and small) and execution and the 'mad riot of the tom tom' (as Lutyens mordantly described most of the work of later British architects in India before his own . . .) continues inside. As the station was also the headquarters of the GIPR (now Central Railways), the interior was required to reflect the prestige of its illustrious board, with massive polished columns hauled from Aberdeen to line the staircase, and a wealth of fine detail in the stained glass and tiles. The object of a daily pilgrimage by millions, VT is a cathedral indeed.

The first foreboding of the Grand Imperial Design ought to have been felt by the Nawab of Oudh, Sadat Aly Khan, when in 1815 he commissioned a cast-iron road bridge for his capital at Lucknow. All the ingredients of the forthcoming technological storm were there: the bridge was designed by John Rennie, who had never been to India; it was made in 2,607 pieces by the Butterley Company of Ripley, Derbyshire, from whence it was shipped to Lucknow; it was an invaluable help to the English during the Lucknow Siege; and, most ignominiously, it still stands, unchanged except by a little widening in the 1960s. Paid for by an Indian ruler, designed at a distance, manufactured in England, shipped halfway round the world in bits, assembled in India, serving a strategic English purpose against those who paid for it, and still

LEFT Victoria Terminus, now officially known as Chhatrapati Shivaji Terminus, but still affectionately called 'VT', is the administrative headquarters of the Central Railway.

RIGHT The Elephant House, Chilham. Built by the father of Sir George Colebrooke, who became Chairman of the East India Company in the 1770s, it was the model for those at Dublin and London zoos. The elephants gained considerable local celebrity, and were visited by Jane Austen.

BELOW Sign on the Grand Trunk Road near Rawalpindi, showing distances all the way to the Afghan border. 'GT1' followed the English progress westwards from Bengal.

going strong – all in all the bridge is as fine a paradigm of the Empire as could be found. Had anyone but noticed the fact that the English were able to cater to the Nawab's commission was truly a clear statement of intent; and, when by 1863 the British had shipped over three million tons of railway lines and steam locomotives to India, they were simply following the technology transfer model set by the bridge over the Gumpti at Lucknow.

In fairness, the traffic in heavy engineering equipment was not entirely one-sided. In 1740 a gentleman living near Canterbury, built the Elephant House, a unique pachydermic stable designed to house elephants brought back from India to help with the clearance of his oak forests, complete with living quarters for the mahouts above.

Francis Hastings, the Governor-General of India between 1813 and 1823, was the first of the improving Governor-Generals. He put into action a number of schemes, including refurbishing irrigation canals and tanks, and built several hundred miles of new roads. Subsequently, the pace quickened considerably, and the first significant contribution of the British to the decayed road system of India was that of consolidating the various sections of the neglected major north Indian artery created by their Imperial predecessors, the Moghuls, and other Indian rulers. The Grand Trunk Road was started in 1839; it was coordinated from Allahabad and ran all the way from Calcutta in the east, 1,500 miles to Peshawar in the west. The scale of the enterprise was mind-boggling as dilapidated sections had to be joined up by new bridges,

GRAND TRUNK ROAD

TAXILA	27 KM		MARDAN	153 KM
WAH	35 //		MANGORA (SWAT)	200 //
HASSANABDAL	47 //		HARIPUR	56 //
ATTOCK	82 //		ABBOTTABAD	116 //
NOWSHERA	114 //		KAGHAN	256 //
PESHAWAR	167 //		MUZAFFARABAD	145 //
KOHAT	176 //		TORKHUM	220 //
RISALPUR	136 //		KABUL	393 //

tunnels and cuttings. The whole road was raised a few feet on rock foundations to prevent flooding during the rains, and then it was metalled. The 250-mile section from Lahore to Peshawar alone required 60,000 people to build the road and its attendant 550 bridges. A supporting cast of rest houses, post offices, police stations and milestones beat regular time for the traveller. Immortalised in Kipling's *Kim*, the Grand Trunk Road remains to this day the principal highway of the subcontinent, although the gentle plod of the bullock cart, or brisk clip-clop of the tonga has largely given way to the noisy, belching roar of the diesel engine or whine of a motorbike. It was completed in ample time for the Mutiny, enabling treacherous (noble) pandies to march quickly to Delhi from Meerut with the noble (treacherous) movable column under John Nicholson hot on their heels.

By 1850, Bombay was connected to Calcutta by a metalled road which is still in existence, and when the English annexed the Punjab after the Second Sikh War in 1849 they were swift to swaddle it in new-built roads – 1,500 miles were completed within three years, with a further 3,000 miles in progress. Road building, although never the favoured pastime of the Empire, was an intrinsic part of the process of absorption and control.

As a result of the railways, time arrived early in India. The English adopted local time practices initially resulting in esoteric variables, all meticulously recorded in almanacks, such as 'Madras moon mean time', 'apparent time' and 'sun at apparent noon'. However, a reliable national railway timetable was not feasible when local times were determined with more or less accuracy by the rising and setting of the sun. Consequently, the whole of India adopted Madras time, and accurate clocks were installed in the station masters' offices to be wound and polished with the respect due to the arbiter of the stopping and starting of steam trains. The invention of time zones for the globe by Sir Stanford Fleming in 1878 was thus readily adopted in India, and the subcontinent became united under one mighty zone of time, far broader than the 15 degrees of longitude suggested by Sir Stanford, but, as the country was under one rule, it hardly seemed to matter. Continental Europe remained chaotic by comparison. The despotic imposition of time is a peculiarly Imperial trait, still evident in China today, which ought to have five time zones and in fact has one. The subcontinent, post-Partition, has acquired a somewhat undecided relationship to time: Pakistan is five hours earlier than GMT, India five and a half hours and Bangladesh six hours. It is as if the warring neighbours wanted to distance themselves from each other symbolically, but were unwilling really to tear themselves more than half an hour away. The effect of train timetables and the concomitant necessity of the observation of clocks, all dutifully imposed by the inflexible sahib, can only be guessed at in a region where still today visitors comment on the apparent abundance of that scarcest of commodities, time.

Telegraph & Post

The telegraph had a brilliant career in India, once again down to the foresight of Dalhousie. Although it had only emerged under the auspices of Morse in America in 1844, by 1857 he could claim to have been responsible for the establishment of 4,000 miles of telegraph lines, enabling news of the outbreak of the Mutiny in Meerut to be conveyed to Agra. 'The cavalry has risen,' wrote Kate Morse to her father 'having killed and wounded all the European soldiers they could find near the lines. If aunt intends starting tomorrow evening, please detain her from doing so, as the van has been prevented from leaving the station.' The end of the Mutiny was signalled in monumental style in one of the first cables successfully transmitted by Reuters on the newly inaugurated transatlantic telegraph on 27 August 1858. 'Emperor of France returned to Paris. King of Prussia too ill to visit Queen Victoria. Settlement of Chinese question. Gwalior insurgent army broken up. All India becoming tranquil.' A subsequent telegraph from London halted the redeployment of two regiments from Nova Scotia to India, saving the Government an estimated £10,000 in costs – the technology had quickly proved its worth. By 1870, the process of wiring up the Empire was complete when the first direct telegraph from London to Calcutta was inaugurated, a year after the opening of the Suez Canal.

The Mutiny occurred at a strange technological interregnum in India; whilst the railways extended for only 150 miles prior to the outbreak, the telegraph was already in full swing. Thus Kate Morse's private message gave the new Governor-General, George Canning, a thousand miles away in Calcutta, the first inkling of trouble, but there was little railway with which to speed reinforcements. Had the Mutiny taken place but ten years later, much of the Ganges Valley, where most of the disturbances took place, would have been accessible by rail, and it is unlikely that the insurrection would have lasted so long. Whilst they have been superseded in the West for many years, telegrams form a vital part of the communications system in India even today, being efficient and affordable. They are under threat from the ubiquitous e-mail, to which the Indians have taken like buffaloes to water.

The introduction of the telegraph coincided with that of the Uniform Postal Service, another of Dalhousie's engines of social progress. The uniform refers less to the attire of the postal workers than to the fact that from 1855 a letter could be sent anywhere from anywhere in India for half an anna – a very small amount, but nonetheless sufficient to enable the postal service to make an operating profit. Prior to Dalhousie's reforms, working out the postal rate for a letter from, say, Bombay to Peshawar required lengthy consultation with a daunting book of tables. A network of post offices and letter boxes was established along British lines, and the legacy of Dalhousie's initiative survives today.

OPPOSITE LEFT **A Victorian letterbox still in use in Calcutta.**

OPPOSITE RIGHT **Returned to sender.**

POST

Irrigation

The building of irrigation canals in India, especially in the Indo-Gangetic plains, predated Moghul times, but the British raised the game to undreamed levels. The issue was principally that of finding a way of dealing with the all-too-frequent outbreaks of famine, and the answer lay in 'trains and drains' as far as the administration was concerned. Lord Ripon, Viceroy between 1880 and 1884, wrote of the Famine Commission: '(It seemed to him) almost a test question for the English Government in India – a test of whether or not it is beneficial to the country. If with all our power and all our knowledge and all our science we cannot preserve them from dying of starvation by hundreds of thousands every few years, how can we justify our domination over them?' Whilst detractors of British Imperialism see the railway initiative merely as a way for British goods to reach new markets, it is less easy to view the irrigation of India with such cynicism. Indeed, the statue raised in Andhra Pradesh to Sir Arthur Cotton in 1987 provoked the remark: 'It is not commonplace for a nation recently relieved of government by foreigners to erect a statue in honour of one of them.' Major-General Cotton had initiated and supervised the building of dams and irrigation canals in the Khrisna, Cauvery and Godavari basins in the 1840s.

In the eighteenth century, the English emphasis had been laid on restoring the irrigation canals and reservoirs left by previous occupants, such as the Moghuls, of lands the Company had recently acquired; later, more ambitious projects such as Cotton's were initiated. By the time the Company had annexed the Punjab in 1849, the Imperial machine was quick to swing into action, and the Upper Bari Doab canal project, designed to 'vivify and regenerate the wildest wastes' of the districts around Amritsar and Lahore, was begun. This played no small role in convincing the Punjabis that the Company was a more benign Raj than that of the capricious Ranjit Singh.

The famine of 1837, which led to the death of over 800,000 people in the Ganges and Jumna valleys, led to the first major irrigation project using waters of the sacred Ganges. Lord Auckland, the then Governor-General, saw the starvation at first hand, and his sister, the diarist Emily Eden, recorded: 'You cannot conceive the horrible sights we see, particularly children; perfect skeletons in many cases, their bones through their skin, without a rag of clothing, and utterly unlike human creatures . . .' Auckland approved an evaluation of a hugely ambitious scheme, put forward by Colonel John Colvin of the Bengal Engineers, for an irrigation canal. When it opened some twenty years later, the Ganges Canal was regarded as a modern wonder of the world, the largest engineering project of its kind ever undertaken. The works started in 1851 by the Ganges near Hardwar, rather unsuccessfully employing the services of the steam

LEFT Pakistan, North West Frontier Province. One of the many irrigation canals built by the British, an ubiquitous feature of north Indian village life.

train Thomason, the first seen on the subcontinent. As befitting anything to do with Mother Ganga, the project required the approval of the Brahmin community, which was obtained by the building of new bathing ghats and rest houses. Large stone lions mark a suitably Imperial junction of the river with the canal, which then flows for a further 800 miles across the previously arid countryside, with another 2,000 miles of feeder canals.

British-built irrigation canals are still very much a feature of subcontinental life, particularly in Pakistan and Indian Punjab. The Indus River is punctuated by six vast barrages (four predating Partition), which divert the waters out of the river itself into large canals which disperse in an ever-finer web into the countryside. If rivers are the veins of the earth, then irrigation canals are its artificial arteries, returning life-giving water to the parched lands that nature neglected. The economically vital cotton crop of the Pakistan Punjab is only possible as a result of irrigation.

River Ferries

An inhabitant of the British Isles rarely experiences a ferry except as a means of leaving in them for fairer climes, whereas the size of the subcontinent's rivers make the ferry a regular feature of getting about, particularly in the East. Scarcely a year passes without a news story of an overloaded passenger ferry sinking with enormous loss of life, tragedies of a scale that would cause ministerial resignations if they happened in the West. Although more and more bridges are being built to cope with the ever-increasing volumes of car, bus and truck traffic, river ferries are still a vital cog in the public transport machine, and are among the surprisingly enduring remains of the Raj. It is not uncommon to see the engine casings marked with the name of some long-defunct manufacturer from Birmingham or Greenock, a reminder that the British Empire in India provided the home country with one of its largest export markets.

Before the advent of improved roads and railways, rivers were often the easiest way for the English to travel, and were also the main commercial arteries. As the Company's territories expanded in Bengal, the Ganges was used for those travelling up the country from Calcutta, often in the comparative luxury of a large boat equipped with sails and oarsmen. The coming of steamships eased the opening up, via the Brahmaputra, of the new tea plantations in Assam. The Indus, at the opposite end of the subcontinent, was served by a regular steamship from Karachi to Multan, the first-class fare in 1854 being 200 rupees. Although the railways largely supplanted the rivers as the highways of the land, rivers still needed to be crossed; and steel-plate ferries, crude in shape and structure, and powered by great diesel engines from the British industrial heartlands, still carry people, goats, bicycles, cotton bales, sacks of rice and indeterminate bundles in crowded, colourful confusion.

RIGHT **A typical subcontinental river scene, with the old British-built ferry moored near traditional wooden craft.**

Lines on the Map

The concept of Empire developed hand in hand with the ability of Western science to forward it: political science to extol the benefits; social science to justify the subjugation of the poor and ignorant in the name of advancement and justice; economic science to promote the importance of free trade; engineering to forge it together; hydrology to irrigate it and theology to demonstrate its religious necessity. However, no science was more important than that of cartography. Blake's vision of Newton measuring the universe with dividers was manifest in the huge advances made by Europeans in their ability to quantify the imponderables of the oceans and continents. Maps not only defined the Empire, but largely facilitated it.

Britannia's ruling of the waves relied not just on formidable naval firepower, but a systematic measuring of the oceans, their currents, tides, winds, shoals, reefs, depths and seasonal weather patterns. The East India Company's formation had been partly inspired by the charts stolen by van Linschoten and partly due to the creation of a fully-fledged trading network in the East, made possible, and woven together, by the advances in oceanography and navigation over the following two hundred years. Valuable ships, and their yet more valuable cargoes, could sink ignominiously as a result of an uncharted shallow or an unexpected rip tide.

Not surprisingly, from the earliest days a ship's captain was charged with the responsibility of measuring and recording every minutiae of his passage, having been trained to sketch and report as he sailed into unknown seas. The captain's log was of vital interest, not only because it recorded the details of the trades undertaken, but because of its usefulness to future mariners. The loss of a ship was one thing; the loss of the record of how and where a ship was sunk was quite another. It is remarkable how often the captain's log survived even the most disastrous wreck; clutched, wrapped in oilskin, in the hands of a dying mariner to be picked up months later from a god-forsaken beach. The Company employed an oceanographer, William Dalrymple, to chart the eastern seas when the highways of England were still only delineated by vague representations of their rude and rutted passage across that country.

Whilst the charting of the oceans proceeded apace, the mapping of the land mass of the Indian subcontinent, like that of England, remained at best haphazard. What did it matter exactly how far Bombay was from Madras by land, when a sea voyage was the only practical way of getting between the two? Plassey and the conquest of Bengal changed all that. The revenues, or Diwani of Bengal ceded to Clive, were based on land taxes. Major James Rennell, having been appointed to Surveyor-General of Bengal by Clive in 1764, produced a survey in 1778 as a means of validating, quantifying and thereby assuring that income. As with its medieval

RIGHT **Mount Everest which lies on the Nepal/Tibet border. Its height was first accurately plotted by cartographers from British India, who claimed it as a record and named it after their Surveyor-General.**

predecessor, *The Domesday Book*, a systematic survey had to be made of a country in order to gather its full bounty. In 1783 Rennell produced the first reasonably accurate map of India: *Memoir of a Map of Hindoostan*.

Once the British had flexed their cartographical muscles, they set about mapping India with a prescience that outraced even their voracious appetite for new territories. The trigonometrical mapping of the Great Arc, an unprecedented scientific exercise which took fifty years, started innocently enough after the fall of Tipu Sultan of Mysore in 1799. A taciturn Yorkshireman called William Lambton managed to persuade an eminently persuadable Richard Wellesley – then Governor-General and the great exponent of the 'Forward Policy' – that, in addition to the conventional topographical survey of Mysore, then being undertaken by Colin Mackenzie, he should start a trigonometrical survey of stupendous accuracy. Starting with a base line over seven miles long and fifteen feet above sea level near Madras, the meticulous triangulation process set off west to Bangalore, employing a particularly sensitive, and enormously heavy, theodolite.

From there it went south to the very southern most point of India, Cape Cormorin, taking advantage of the recent extension of British influence over the Rajah of Tanjore and the rather less subtle victory by force of arms over the Raja of Travancore. It then headed north through the semi-compliant lands of the Sultan of Hyderabad. Various members of the survey team were killed by tigers, attacked by bandits and ravaged by disease. Lambton himself died in Hinganghat, Maharashtra, the victim of exhaustion.

ABOVE **The recently discovered grave of William Lambton, Hinghanghat. The great cartographer omitted to leave his map coordinates for posterity when he died in 1832.**

By the time the Great Arc had reached Mussorie, in the foothills of the Himalayas, some forty years later, it was under the command of the dictatorial George Everest. It had spread its tentacles east to Calcutta, west to Mangalore and Bombay, and along various other lines in the Ganges plain. The problem of finding a suitable high location to place the theodolite in the featureless plains had been solved by the construction of stone towers over sixty feet high, some of which still survive today.

When an actual 'base line' measurement was made of the final hypothetical side of a triangle near Sironj, a discrepancy of just 6.395 inches was found over a distance of seven and a quarter miles. The Great Arc had crawled its way 1,500 miles north up the centre of the subcontinent, and was accurate to less than the width of a chapati.

This monumental feat of mapping had the unforeseen consequence of providing an accurate measure of the altitude of Himalaya Peak XV, a distant massif beyond the more obviously imposing peak of Kanjenjunga in Nepal. Although the British had not conquered Nepal, their

ABOVE Lambton's great Theodolite, which allowed the British to map their Indian Empire. It is preserved with pride at the Survey of India Offices.

theodolites and measuring instruments were able to penetrate far beyond its borders, and proclaim Peak XV, at 29,028 feet, the highest in the world. From their distant viewing point they appropriated the mountain, and named it Mount Everest, after the irascible head of the Indian Survey who had made the measurement possible.

The mapping of the Indian subcontinent, whilst not specifically Imperial in conception, had specifically Imperial effects. Without accurate topographical surveys, metalled roads, railways and irrigation canals could not be built. Previously uncharted rivers could now be opened for traffic and all-important trade, and treaties could be signed with precise territorial meaning.

LEFT The remains of Sir George Everest's house in Park Estate, near the hill station of Mussoorie. He lived there from 1832 until 1843 whilst he was in charge of the Great Trigonometrical Survey of India.

When Partition became inevitable, small districts of the Punjab assumed enormous importance in the division between India and Pakistan, and hundreds of thousands may be said to have died because they were caught on the wrong side of a line on the map.

The decision of the Hindu ruler of predominantly Muslim Kashmir to join India at Partition continues to bring two nuclear powers to the brink of mutually assured destruction, and their armies face each other across one of the highest valleys in the world. The Great Game is no longer played by the British, but their inheritors have adopted the game enthusiastically, including the playground. In fact, the whole Kashmir question was brought about by a poor English decision. The ending of the First Sikh War with the Treaty of Lahore in 1845 meant that the Company, whilst not actually annexing the Punjab, had imposed strict conditions on the future running of the Kingdom, and installed Political Agents to ensure that their will was executed. One of the treaty's clauses made provision for substantial war reparations, and the British Resident in Lahore, Henry Lawrence, was concerned that the Company received its money. In an uncharacteristically high-handed move, he suggested that Kashmir, belonging to the Sikhs but run by a Muslim, Sheikh Imam-ud-Din, be sold to Maharajah Gulab Singh, the Hindu ruler of neighbouring Jammu. This was highly unpopular with the Kashmiri Muslims, and the Company had to send in a 10,000 man army to enforce their decision. The Company was thus paid its reparations, but the cost of that unjust decision is still borne today.

Partition was the ultimate corollary of the Imperial process: the subcontinent, after thousands of years of waxing and waning empires, kingdoms, fiefdoms, tribes and gangs, had been united cartographically, politically and socially, guided by the remorseless measurements of the British mapmakers. When the time came to leave, the Empire builders relied on their maps once more to dismember it.

The Survey of India still exists, along with its neighbouring equivalents, and they still produce maps of outstanding technical proficiency. Owing to military paranoia, most of these are unavailable to the general public, who must by law be content with maps of a scale no larger than 1:250,000.

LEFT The Survey of India Offices are still where the British left them in Dehra Dun, and their equivalents flourish in Pakistan and Bangladesh.

VI

REST & PLAY

A detail of the fine stonework in the Red Fort, Delhi. The British knocked some of it down to make room for a barracks.

Hill stations

The topography of the subcontinent is amply endowed with upward protrusions, from the unrivalled Himalayas of the north to the Eastern and Western Ghats of the peninsula, and the innumerable lesser ranges between. Not surprisingly, when the English found that their expansion across the wealthy and fertile plains had brought them hard up against these mountains, they started to conjure 'a green thought in a green shade' to avail themselves, in a small way, of God's own air-conditioning in the hills. It was noted that the high incidence of cholera that bedevilled armies was substantially reduced at higher altitude, and convalescence in a hill sanatoria was a considerably cheaper option than sending soldiers home. As was often the case in India, the English could combine pleasure with strategic and economic necessity. As Emily Eden, sister of the Governor-General Lord Auckland, remarked of Simla: 'Like meat, we keep better here.'

For the civilian, the English had built splendid Presidency cities with their English clubs, churches, fine neoclassical town houses and suburban villas, but there was still no relief from the Indian climate. They invented the bungalow and veranda for the Mofussil (areas outside the Presidencies) which, when augmented with punkhas (fans) and tatties (dampened screens), provided a vaguely liveable solution to the problem of the searing heat. However, every collector, district officer, indigo planter and his wife yearned for the cool, airy, damp days of home. The hill station was an answer to that prayer, and the railways made the escape there possible for hitherto unimaginable numbers. From 1864, for six months a year the effective capital of India, home to the Viceroy and the Commander-in-Chief, was not Delhi but an healthful little Himalayan mountain resort called Simla which was 7,000ft and over two hundred miles further north. Even if the men had to remain at work in the sweltering plains, the women could cheerfully become 'grass widows' in a fashionable hill station, where the frisson of scandal might add considerably to its charms.

RIGHT **The hill station of Darjeeling is also the centre of a flourishing tea-growing area. Tea was introduced there by the East India Company's Superintendent, Dr Cambell, shortly after the district was annexed in 1839.**

Simla started as a mountain retreat when a Lieutenant Ross built a temporary wooden home there in 1819, followed by Captain Charles Kennedy's more permanent log cabin in 1822. Lord Amherst declared it a 'vice-regal sanitarium' in 1827, after which its success was assured. Christchurch, the church on the Ridge promenade, was begun in 1844 and the other appurtenances of British life followed – the library, the town hall, and the post office with a fashionable Mall to contain them. The Gaiety Theatre, built in 1887, was the scene of the kind of amateur dramatics that have become a clichéd image of Raj life. The elegant and grand Viceregal Lodge, built in 1888 by Lord Dufferin, now houses the Indian Institute of Advanced Studies. It looks across to Snowdon, the former residence of many Commanders-in-Chief. From these two buildings the fate of a fifth of the planet was determined, over games of tennis in the electric-lit, indoor court of the Lodge, or over cheroots in the billiard room of Snowdon. Lesser mortals stayed at the Cecil Hotel, or at one of the other smaller hotels or boarding

OPPOSITE ABOVE The Viceregal Lodge, Simla. Built in a Scottish baronial style which loosely accords with the pine-forested hills. Its cast iron exterior drain cover came from Kilmarnock.

LEFT The Supreme India Council determines the fate of fifth of the planet at Simla, 'the cradle of more political insanity than any place within the limits of Hindustan'. Raj luminaries include Lord Lawrence, (seated centre), C-in-C Sir Hugh Rose (seated left) and Lord Napier of Magdala (seated right of Lawrence).

OPPOSITE BELOW The Mall, Simla. The Gaiety Theatre can be glimpsed in the background.

houses, many of which are still thriving, as Simla has reinvented itself as Shimla and is one of the leading resort towns of India. It wasn't until 1903 that the railways finally reached Simla itself, and passengers who had previously alighted at Kalka fifty miles away no longer had to endure a tonga ride; nowadays the spectacular narrow-gauge railway journey is one of the principal tourist attractions.

Simla was the pre-eminent hill station, and the formula proved so successful that by the end of the century there were over eighty of them scattered amongst the hills of the subcontinent. Nearly all of them had their mall for shopping and promenading, their botanical gardens for instruction and pleasure, and their cinema for entertainment. Ootacamund was established at over 7,000ft in the Nilgiri Hills by John Sullivan, the Collector of Coimbatore, who had heard of the locality's teeming game and English climate. He built himself the Stone House in 1823, which still survives, and soon the hill station attracted fashionable visitors from Madras, earning it the sobriquet 'Snooty Ooty'. He started importing plants and trees such as strawberries and eucalyptus, made an artificial lake, and became so enamoured of his new venture that he was reprimanded for neglecting his official duties in Coimbatore. Ootacamund was eventually to become the official summer capital of the Madras Presidency, and the area became a centre of tea, coffee and chichona planting. Its botanical gardens were founded in 1848, and the Gymkhana Golf Club by the turn of the century. Ooty's greatest claim to residual Raj influence must be the Ooty Hunt, founded in 1844 and said to be the only hunt between Italy and Australia. Although the quarry is jackal, in every other particular it closely resembles the English model; the horses and pack of hounds are maintained by the army at the nearby Wellington Barracks and the opening meet is at the Fernhill Hotel, the former

BELOW The Dining Room at Chapslee Hotel, one of the oldest houses in Simla. In the 1830s it was used as offices for the viceroy staff. It eventually became the summer residence of the Maharajah of Kapurthala, whose family now run it as a hotel.

ABOVE Hill stations were frequently the sites of breweries, as with this one at Solan on the way to Simla. A sundowner or two helped to oil the great engine of Empire.

residence of the Maharajah of Mysore. All the gentlemen wear pink, there is an annual hunt ball where officers appear in full dress uniform, and the hunt dinner is held at Ooty Club, where photographs of past masters are ranged along the walls. The hunt even holds an annual point-to-point on the downs near the race course.

As well as being healthier for people, the hill stations were free of the wild yeast strains which were prone to frustrate attempts to brew beer in the plains. As a result, many breweries sprang up in the hills, and even in non-drinking Pakistan the brewery at Murree still produces a fine beer. Likewise, many of the schools which clustered around the hill stations remain in service, and although the annual migration of the Great White Sahib no longer takes place, many are sustained by local tourism, and the smattering of western visitors appreciate their nostalgia-ridden charms. Old Dharamsala, the hill station for Lahore before Partition changed its name to McLeodganj after an earthquake forced its residents to move lower down the mountain in 1905. The deserted town has found new life as the home of the Dalai Lama and other exiled Tibetans with libraries, schools, temples and monasteries. Regardless of their current usage, however, the fundamental lure of the hill station as a retreat from the heat still remains. Many of the English homes survive – charming cottages with appropriately English names such as Rose Bower and Dingly Dell. The hill stations, with their cool, bright air and copious greenery, cottages and church bells, were the places in India where even those English who had never been to England could assuage their nostalgia for it.

BELOW The Savoy Hotel, Mussoorie. It was the largest purpose-built hill station hotel in India, and opened in time for a royal visit in May 1906 by HRH the Princess of Wales.

RIGHT Rosemount Hotel, Ranikhet, Uttar Pradesh.

Sport

There's a breathless hush in the Close tonight
Ten to make and the match to win
A bumping pitch and a blinding light,
An hour to play and the last man in,
And it's not for the sake of a ribboned coat,
Or the selfish hope of a season's fame,
But his captain's hand on his shoulder smote
'Play up! Play up! and play the game!'. . .

The sand of the desert is sodden red,
Red with the wreck of the square that broke,
The Gatling's jammed and the Colonel dead,
And the regiment blind with dust and smoke.
The river of death has brimmed his banks,
And England's far, and honour a name,
But the voice of a schoolboy rallies the ranks:
'Play up! Play up! And play the game!'

Sir Arthur Newbolt, '*Vitae Lampada*'

The British invented the current forms of soccer, rugby, cricket, lawn tennis, hockey, badminton, horse racing, and boxing – and snooker, which was invented in Ootacamund Club in 1875. It was partly because of the ubiquity of the Empire, partly because games were an important aspect of the British character-building process, and principally because of an uncanny British genius for striking the right balance between strict rules and freedom of expression in sport, that they have thrived around the world. The ability to achieve this balance may have been in itself an expression of the 'freeborn' Englishman's treasured rights of individual freedom from state interference, protected by a law based on the precedence whereby justice and fair play were the underlying principles. Rules of games, as with laws, were in this context subservient to a governing principle of fairness. An action can be within the rules but it is still 'not cricket' if it breaches the higher, unwritten protocol. For the English, in sport, as in life, the notion of a gentleman was not simply a matter of adherence to the rules, but an instinctive understanding of their guiding morality. As the Empire matured, such ideals were reflected by English sports. 'In the history of the British Empire it is written that England has

previous page The Esplanade, Bombay. Cricket matches in progress: despite the players' whites, the state of the outfield is noticeably informal. Results can be quickly relayed to *The Times of India* building on the right.

right The racecourse, Bombay. The English exported their passion for racing throughout the Empire, and pictures of the most successful Indian racehorses were hung in East India House in London.

owed her sovereignty to her sports.' wrote J. E. C. Wheldon, Bishop of Calcutta and Headmaster of Harrow 1885–98. In a world where sport is a huge industry, its participants have become superstars, its media coverage is gargantuan and its drug and corruption problems only slightly less so, it is salutary to reflect on the innocence of the amateur ideal in sport, and its correspondence with the ideals of the British Empire.

However, cricket, the most successful export to India, did not start its life as innocently as one might expect. It was a game played by gentlemen using hirelings from the lower orders, and the rules were first written down in order that gambling on the outcome would be more viable. Corruption, bribery and match-throwing were even more common then than today. However, the game gradually evolved into something which exemplified higher ideals: manliness, fair play, and the ability to treat the 'twin impostors' of victory and defeat with equanimity. It arrived in India in 1721, played by the officers and crew of an English ship. It was taken up with alacrity in the three Presidencies, and the Calcutta Cricket Club was formed in 1792. The game was confined to the English for most of the next century, and although the Parsees in Bombay formed the Oriental Cricket Club in 1848, it was not until the 1880s that they played a match against the British. The creation of schools and universities, and the emergence of an English-speaking Indian elite, gave the game wider exposure; it was thought that if the natives were to be exposed to Western thought and culture, cricket should be an essential part of the curriculum. Then India produced the first of its cricketing heroes, the Maharajah Sir Ranjitsinhi Vibhaji of Nawangar, whose batsmanship exhibited a wide improvisational streak that caught the imagination of English and Indians alike. 'Ranji', a Cambridge Blue, 'moved as if he had no bones', and saved England against Australia in 1899. Partly inspired by him, by the early twentieth century cricket had in effect become the national game, and since 1934 the Ranji Trophy has been the most important domestic cricket prize.

The Independence movement did nothing to dampen the subcontinent's enthusiasm for the game; whilst many aspects of Britishness were reviled by the Nationalists as cultural impositions, cricket appears somehow to have escaped their attention. Since Partition, matches between Pakistan and India have become increasingly 'war by other means', and matches can disappear in clouds of tear-gas and battles with riot police. Both these nations have gone from strength to strength on the world cricketing stage along with the 'white colonies' of Australia, New Zealand and South Africa. The 'mother country' (literally, as least as far as cricket is concerned) has struggled on, each much-heralded revival of English cricket fizzling out like a mishit drive in dew-laden grass. Attendance at matches in England continues to fall, teams are made up of time-serving professionals and public interest wanes, whilst on the subcontinent the game is as vibrant and well-supported as ever. The modest cricketing ideals that underpinned the game have largely withered on the vine, and a new breed of the media-hip cricketing celebrity struts upon the stage.

From the other games in the British sporting catalogue, India has selected hockey. Originally it was played by the Anglo-Indian community in the railway towns where they tended to congregate, which differentiated them from the British and the natives, reinforcing their own identity. As the Anglo-Indian has become a dying breed, hockey has become more mainstream. Again, teams from Pakistan and India compete consistently at the highest international level, whilst the English national teams make a sporadic impact. There seems to be an unavoidable connection between the decline of the British Empire and the decline of British sporting prowess; the nation's last great collective sporting achievement, football's 1966 World Cup victory, aptly took place in the former Empire Stadium, Wembley. The renaming of that stadium was a conscious rejection of an outmoded national, and perhaps sporting ideal.

LEFT The banks of the Mula River, Maharashtra. As once was the case in England, cricket is played on every conceivable pitch.

Hunting

In common with their other colonies, the decimation of the local wildlife in India was considered a British *droit de seigneur*. Whilst their Moghul predecessors were no slouches in this department, the British dragged the slaughter to new depths, and it is an agonising glimpse of the mindless squandering of nature's wealth to see photographs of Edwardian hunts where twenty-eight tigers had been shot and proudly displayed. Of course, saying this is to be guilty of historical hindsight, as conservation was scarcely part of anybody's consciousness until quite recently, and the notion that tigers could have been nurtured and protected in special preserves would have seemed ridiculous. Today's anglers photographed with their catch would feel much the same. It is questionable whether the tigers, wild boars, deer and birds that were the regular hunting fare of the British would have survived under any other Raj but, in their ruthlessly efficient, well-engineered way, it is certainly hard to imagine anyone better equipped to carry out the carnage.

LEFT Lady 'Vizzy' wife of the Maharaj Kumar Vijaya Anand of Vizianagram in the Durbar Hall of their Palace at Benares, with some of the 315 tigers that her husband shot.

RIGHT The King-Emperor's tiger hunt after the Delhi Durbar, 1911. George V makes a notable contribution to wildlife conservation efforts in his Indian domains.

Clubs

As well as their sporting obsessions, and frequently in parallel to them, the Imperial British have always been renowned for their clubs, and in India the club reached its apogee, becoming simultaneously a home from home and daily reaffirmation of the virtues of fair play and honourable behaviour, and the ultimate expression of the Empire builders' apartheid mentality. The reassuring rustle of newspapers and chiming of a well-wound clock spoke of permanence, standards and an unswerving Britishness – a far cry from the mysterious mayhem of the world which was resolutely kept outside. The more spectacular clubs naturally evolved in the Presidencies, and many are still thriving. However, recondite ones such as the Bombay Lieder Kranz, founded in 1887 'for all gentlemen able to converse in German', and the Ammunition Factory Institute at Dum-Dum have quietly disappeared. Some of the Masonic Lodges, of which there were over fifty throughout India by 1875, still exist. Many of the clubs in the hill stations have preserved their colonial atmosphere more or less intact, as would be expected in an environment that was specifically designed to re-create an ideal of Englishness, but also because their *raison d'etre* is still valid – the Planters Club in Darjeeling is still an important meeting place for the tea community, and it is the official headquarters of the Darjeeling Planters Association. Other clubs serve less worthy, but equally important functions, such the Peshawar Club which is able to sell liquor to foreigners provided that they sign on as a registered alcoholic. It is the only function that the splendid bar, redolent with the ghosts of hard-drinking officers and respectably tipsy memsahibs, is still able to carry out.

RIGHT The Planters Club, Darjeeling. Great stirrings in the world of tea have been witnessed here.

OPPOSITE The Gymkhana Club. Another cricket match in progress.

4

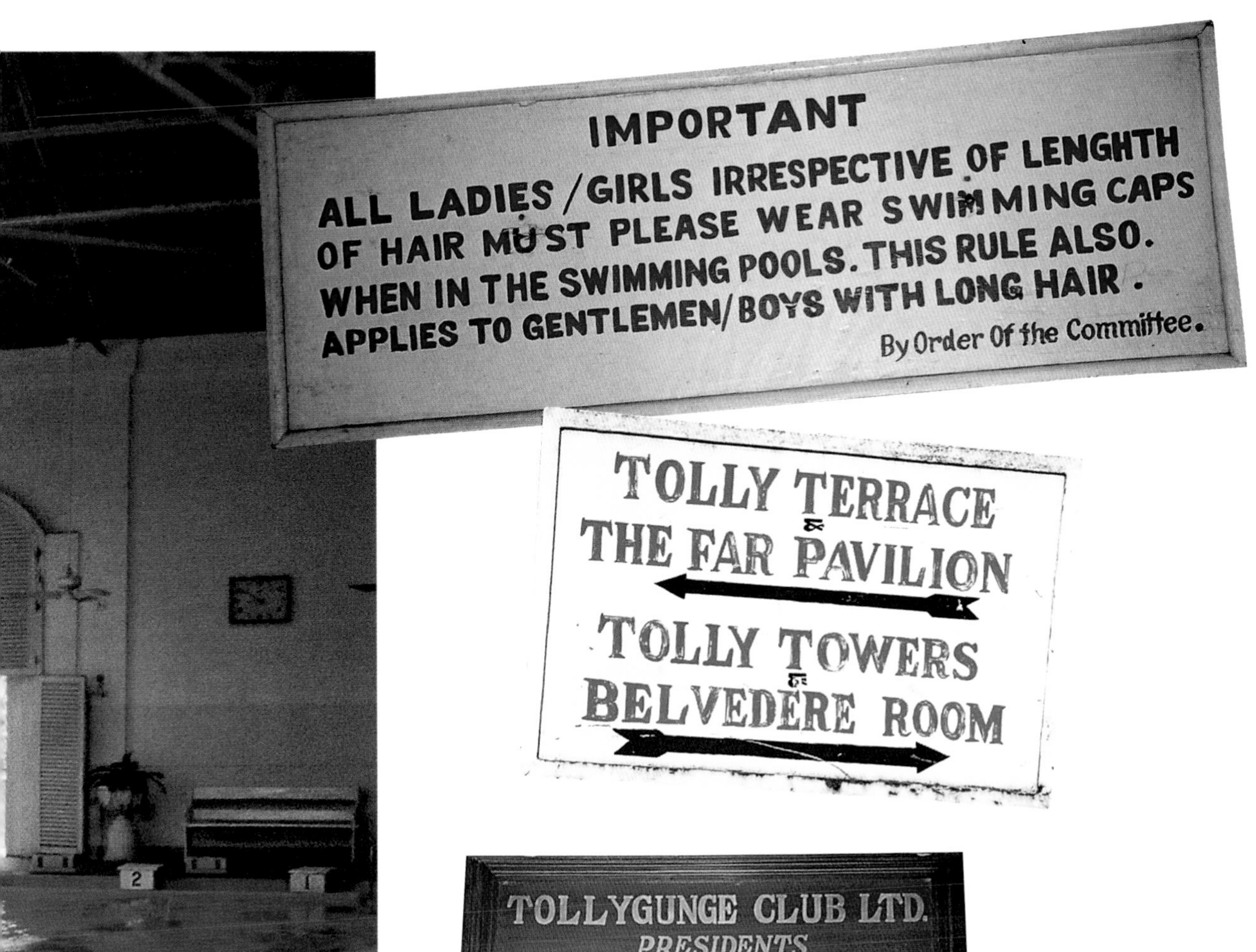

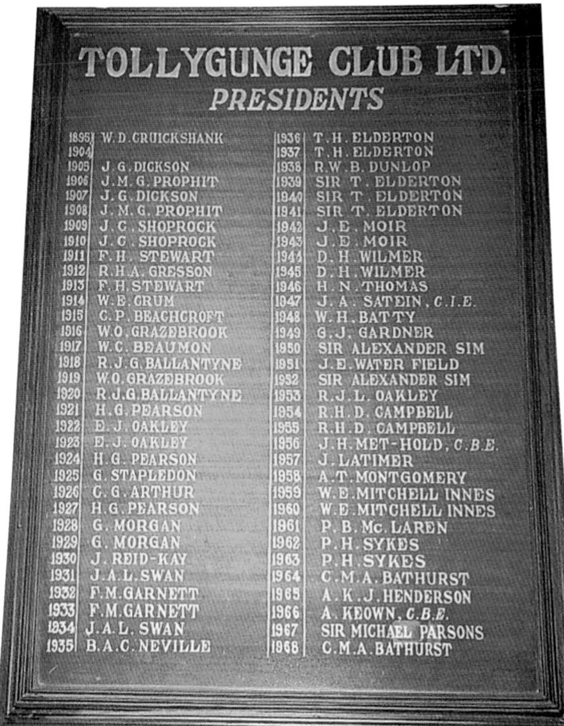

OPPOSITE AND LEFT The Tollygunge Club, Calcutta. Founded in 1895 in the former residence of the deposed sons of Tipu Sultan of Mysore, it is one of the city's most exclusive sporting clubs.

Hotels

The concept of the hotel gathered momentum in tandem with the expansion of the railways and the development of the cantonment and hill station. The oldest hotel in Asia, Spence's in Calcutta, was founded as late as 1830, and prior to that, in cities men used to be put up at 'chummeries', basic bachelor accommodation, and Government rest houses or 'dak' (post) bungalows provided for travelling officials. These are still found throughout the subcontinent, and are often the most comfortable places to stay in remote districts. The rest houses provided for the Forestry Service and the Archaeological Service are frequently found in spectacular locations. At Vijayanagar, for example, there is one built inside a fourteenth-century Hindu temple, and its architecture combines serendipitously with the venerable 1930s plumbing. In the princely state of Hyderabad, the largest cantonment on the subcontinent at Secunderabad spawned a suitably impressive hotel, the Deccan, for the temporary accommodation of the Indian Army officers who inevitably found themselves there at some stage during their careers.

Anglo-Indians often went in for the hotel trade, as it offered them the opportunity to be close to the European milieu if not exactly part of it. A number of small family-run hotels still survive, although many have yielded to the inevitable commercial pressure to sell their spacious city-centre properties. Dean's in Peshawar, a delightful turn-of-the-century hotel with bungalows dotted around shady gardens, has succumbed only recently, continuing in a much truncated form. Despite the influx of the global chains with all mod-cons, some of the hotels from the Raj era, such as the Metropole in Karachi, retain a certain social cachet. The landmark Taj Mahal Hotel in Bombay, built on the waterfront by the Indian-owned Tata Company at the beginning of the last century, is still viewed as a quintessential remnant of the Raj. The fortunes of the most prestigious hotel chain in India were established by the shrewd purchase of a formerly British-owned hotel. Raibahadur Oberoi bought the lease on the Grand Hotel in Calcutta in 1938, and later acquired the Maidens in Delhi and the Cecil in Simla, forming the Oberoi Hotel Group.

RIGHT The Taj Mahal Hotel, Apollo Bunder, Bombay. Built in the early 1900s by the Tata family, it has since been Bombay's premier hotel, with its matchless view of the Gateway of India.

Newspapers

The newspapers in India are often of British origin: the literate native population of India was, and still frequently is, literate in English. However, the papers were far from being the organs of Government. The first newspaper, the *Bengal Gazette* founded in 1780, was closed down by Warren Hastings, and James Augustus Hicky, its editor, was imprisoned. Subsequently, the name was revived for the first newspaper for Indians in Bengali, in 1818. A number of such papers sprang up which addressed a limited readership, usually with a business bias. By the late nineteenth century, the educational strategies of the previous thirty years bore fruit as Indian newspapers written in English started to take advantage of the new technologies such as Reuters and the telegraph, and frequently to voice an anti-British, pro-Nationalist line. Once the struggle for independence was decided, many newspapers lost their political impetus, and the original British stalwarts regained ground – *The Times of India* founded 1838 and *The Statesman*, founded 1875. In Pakistan, the old British newspapers could not survive the new Islamic regime, and the *Kurrachee Advertiser* founded in 1845 and the *Koh-e Nur*, founded in 1850 – an Urdu newspaper from Lahore – died away, to be replaced by the formerly Delhi based *Dawn* (in English) and *Jang* (in Urdu). In East Pakistan, previously unpressed, a post-Partition English-language paper, the *Bangladesh Observer*, was founded in 1949, but the movement for separation from Pakistan was supported by the *Ittefuq*. Neither in Pakistan or what is now Bangladesh has what the West would call a free press flourishing beyond the confines of a particular agenda; whereas in India the tradition of journalistic and editorial freedom has been generally maintained.

LEFT English language newspapers are still a significant national medium.

LEFT *The Times of India* building, Bombay.

Lonely Hearts

In the days of the East India Company Raj, lonely Englishmen from the 'mofussil' (the countryside away from the Presidencies) would frequently despair of finding an English wife, and thus the infamous 'Fishing Fleet' came into being. At its coarsest level, a boatload of the less-than-lady-like sweepings of Bow and Bermondsey would be unloaded in Calcutta to be descended upon by soldiers and lowly clerks in search of a wife. Those who remained unchosen might often end up in a life of squalor in India of which they'd never dreamed when they left England, and although the Company initially sponsored some of the shipments, they quickly found that they were in danger of filling the bazaars with fallen English women. At the more sophisticated end, spinster sisters visiting brothers, widowed nieces visiting uncles and other women lacking fortune or looks, or both, might try their luck in India, where the new-found wealth of the Company's servants made the journey worth the attendant risks of disease and death.

For their part, young or not-so-young men of the mofussil would periodically descend on Calcutta in the hope of finding a match amongst the season's wares. As transportation improved, and home leave became a more realistic option, the market moved back to England, where men would use their few months to track and trap a wife ready for a prompt marriage on their return to India. As Herbert Edwardes urged his friend, the future General John Nicholson, on home leave at the time: 'How good it is for our best purposes to be *helped* by a noble wife, who loves you better than all men and women, but God better than you.' Nicholson was Deputy Commissioner of Bannu in the North West Frontier, as far-flung an outpost of the Empire as could be imagined: however, he remained resolutely a bachelor, in keeping with his lifestyle of remorseless military action, innumerable floggings and self-denying Christianity.

Friends and relatives in the Presidencies or back home were prevailed upon to provide a steady stream of eligible would-be memsahibs, but when they failed, the newspapers provided another vehicle for a bachelor's *cri de coeur*, and so the lonely hearts column was born. Members of the prestigious Indian Civil Service, posted to the back of beyond, could advertise for a wife of the right class, age and general attributes, and readers of *The Times*, or *The Times of India*, could trawl the column for a likely match for their less marriageable female relatives. Letters would be exchanged, a meeting arranged, and if both the parties approved, the Deputy Collector's bungalow at Nowshera would be swiftly provided with a suitable memsahib.

Such marital arrangements, executed through the new medium of newspapers, were an eminently practical way of solving an intractable problem, and although the unabashed exchange of details of class, occupation and financial status would appear *de trop* to a modern

Alliance for very handsome Khatri
BOY, 30/180CM,
B.Com(H), LLB, PGDBM, Executive Director
in foremost group with annual income in seven figure, belonging
status South Delhi family.
If the girl is really
beautiful, slim and fair, around 25 years minimum 160cm,
please send details to marriage coordinator,
Mr. J.K. Malhotra,
UCO Bank Building, 4th floor, Parliament Street, New Delhi.
Phone (O)3718167
(R) 91-5272087

ABOVE AND OPPOSITE
Lonely hearts advertisements. Caste, qualifications, income and horoscopes are all material.

ALLIANCE from tall beautiful Bengali girl below 25 yrs for my son 32/172. Negotiation welcomed from broadminded family of Punjabi, Kashmiri Hindu family. Boy Veg. Asst in Govt job doing MBA. Early simple marriage Mother Brahmin father Kayastha. Language province no bar. Write Box No. PA 9745K Times Of India, Patna-800001.

Alliance for
VERY WELL ESTABLISHED DYNAMIC SMART BOY 31/175 CMS
belonging to high status respectable Srivastav family.
CURRENTLY HEADING INDIAN OPERATION OF A MNC ENGAGED IN FASHION BUSINESS AT DELHI
Caste no bar. Correspond with biodata & photograph to Box No. FAI661R Times Of India, NewDelhi-110002.

WANTED a beautiful brahmin girl preferably Software Engineer/MCA/MBA for smart brahmin boy BE/MBA/26/5'7" working with MNC.Only son of renowned doctor's family own nursing home. Respond with photo biodata horoscope To: Dr.HariOm Sharma Chaudhran ka Bagich PO Guna-473001 MP

SOUTH Indian (Mysore) Brahmin, 48, (born Jan 53), never married, Post- Grad Engg, Senior Computer Exec, MNC, looking for slim, smart vegetarians around 40 or over settled India or abroad. Iyengars/ Vaishnavs/ Krishna devotees most welcome. Email wru9@yahoo.co.in or reply Box No. BBF425X Times Of India, Mumbai-400001.

English audience accustomed to love matches, the system has been adopted in India with a vengeance. As most marriages were traditionally arranged by families, with caste and social standing being of particular importance, the culture of the lonely hearts column is not far removed from previous practice. The oft-repeated desirability of fair skin surprises many westerners, who do not realise that WASP racial prejudices have their subcontinental counterparts, and a white skin is almost invariably regarded as 'prettier', and creams and lotions are widely available to help achieve the desired effect.

In Bombay, a kind of real-life lonely hearts column has been set up in the shadow of the Afghan Church, a large notice board is placed against the railings, decorated with a few suitably matrimonial trimmings, and candidates come and go, shyly posting their advertisement and hoping perhaps for a romantic chance encounter. More blatant in intent, perhaps, but not so different in effect to the balls and banquets of the Calcutta social round two hundred years ago.

सत्यमेव जयते

GOVERNMENT & EDUCATION

The emblem of India has
replaced the Royal Coat of Arms
on the gates to the magnificent
Viceroy's House, New Delhi, now
home to the President of India.

New Delhi

It is perhaps an apt symbol of the vainglory of worldly ambitions that the greatest and most enduring monument to the Raj, built to house its majesty and administration, should be completed only shortly before Britain's hold on India disintegrated. Whilst New Delhi outwardly projects the Raj triumphant, the British were unconsciously building their final memorial. It is the most architecturally coherent, and most pleasing of twentieth-century cities; one which, despite the press of population and pervasive pollution of modern India, retains an extravagant sense of space and elegance. Perhaps too extravagant: the great avenues and axial roads, fine for parades and sweeping ambassadorial limousines, dwarf the pedestrian, and whilst New Delhi's scale has enabled it to absorb the worst of India's traffic relatively unscathed, the individual on foot is overwhelmed. New Delhi remains a fundamentally Imperial statement of exclusivity, privilege and distance conspicuously failing to fit in with the rest of the city and its teeming millions.

Lord Valentia, a friend of the Governor-General Richard Wellesley, remarked that India should be ruled from a palace not a counting house, 'with the ideas of a prince, not those of a retail trader in muslins and indigo'. Until that time, the Governors had lived in houses designed more for comfort than display. It was Wellesley who, encouraged by his friend, built a new Government House in Calcutta modelled on Keddleston Hall in Derbyshire. Completed in 1803, it admirably expressed the transition from the East India Company as a purely trading entity to the Company Raj. However, the £167,359 price tag in part led to Wellesley's recall to England as the Court of Directors were not yet ready to fund such princely ambitions. Lord Curzon, whose ancestral home actually was Keddleston, settled into the eerily familiar surroundings of Government House as Viceroy a hundred years later with the remark that whilst the pillars of the original were made of alabaster, these were made of lath and plaster. Such was the scale of the palace that Lady Dufferin, the wife of an earlier Viceroy, opined vaguely that the kitchens might be found 'somewhere in Calcutta'.

RIGHT **New Delhi, Lutyens' masterpiece, the Rashtrapati Bhavan, the former Viceroy's House.**

The baton of ostentation was picked up in the construction of other government buildings around India, and even in the Princely States. The Residency in Hyderabad was a magnificent building which proclaimed the influence of the British, as personified by the Resident, James Kirkpatrick, who had married a local princess. It did not go unnoticed that the Residency, started in 1803, was paid for by the Nizam himself who was the most powerful of India's independent rulers. Hyderabad was forcibly annexed by India soon after Partition, and the former Residency now enjoys a less exalted existence as home of the University College for Women. By the mid-nineteenth century it was fully accepted that the palaces of the provincial governors and residents were to be an architectural expression of Imperial power. In the form of country retreats, that expression was duplicated, then triplicated with the advent of the hill station. The subcontinent is still speckled with the results of the British rulers' desire to display their power, and thus the political elite in India, Pakistan and Bangladesh have inherited a fine set of gubernatorial palaces and other government buildings, although many have been turned to more public use.

The ultimate corollary of the assertion of Empire through architecture was that British India should have a purpose-built capital, and it was thus that George V declared at the Delhi Durbar of 1911 that a new capital would be built in that city. The 'retailers in muslin and indigo' by whom Calcutta had been founded would give way to the rightful successors of the Moghuls in the most Imperial of Indian cities. Of course, it did not escape the notice of the gainsayers that the reason that Delhi had such a rich Imperial history was that all the successive rulers who had built new cities there – the Moghul Shah Jehan being the last in a long line of seven – had in fairly short order lost their empires. In wilful defiance of the laws of history, Edwin Lutyens and his partner, Herbert Baker, were commissioned to design the last and possibly greatest expression of the Imperial sensibility that the world is likely to see. Delhi had resonances for the British other than its Moghul echoes; the city had been the scene of some of the fiercest fighting in the Mutiny and was littered with memories of fallen heroes. It boasted a perfectly adequate European quarter known as the Civil Lines, built to the north of the Old City of Shahjehanabad on the Ridge from which the infamous Siege had been conducted. That, however, was not considered a suitable location for the projected capital, which required a much broader canvas.

OPPOSITE **New Delhi. The dome of Rashtrapati Bhavan shows off its Buddhist influences.**

The site that was chosen was on the empty plain south of Shahjehanabad. The plan called for an axial ceremonial avenue called Kingsway, two miles long and twice the width of the Champs-Elysée, with elegant canals and shady trees, a monolithic statue of George V and India Gate, a memorial to the soldiers of the Indian Army. At the end of Kingsway, after a small rise in the road which caused some altercation between the two architects (Lutyens wanted to remove it, whereas Baker thought it helped the composition), was to be a palace bigger than Versailles, named, with an affectation of domesticity which was common practice amongst the grander buildings of the Raj, Viceroy's House. Six hundred feet long and nearly two hundred feet high, the house is set on Raisana Hill. It was here that Lutyens, the architect who was hitherto known for his interpretation of the English country house, produced an unexpected masterpiece.

Lutyens was personally something of a Britisher of the 'old school', and managed not only to hold most native Indians but also their architecture in contempt, conceding only grudgingly that some of the Moghul work at Agra was lovely. However, he equally abhorred the 'Indo-Sarcenic-Swiss-Gothic-Wild-West-Italianate' style that the British deployed with varying emphasis in their cities and hill stations, referring to these hybrid effusions as 'the mad riot of tom toms'. He was married to Emily, the daughter of a former Viceroy Lord Lytton, a woman who openly espoused the cause of Indian Independence. Whether this modified his contempt for the vernacular is not recorded, but what is surprising is both the boldness and originality of the architecture of his Viceroy's House. Pressured by the Viceroy, Lord Hardinge, to conform to the 'tom tom' style beloved by the British, and conditioned by his own prejudices to despise native architecture, Lutyens opted for the most unexpected of influences for the composition of the dominant central dome of the house, which was probably based on the Buddhist stupa at Sanchi near Bhopal. Buddhism had ceased to be a religious force in India since the first Muslim invasions a millennium earlier, so the derivation is particularly unexpected. Although classical Greece underpinned the basic proportions and design of the structure, Lutyens included Moghul elements in the details such as 'chattris', or decorative pavilions, and the pierced stone screens. The gardens seemed in part unashamedly Moghul, delighting in fountains and pools, and in part a formal English rose-garden.

RIGHT New Delhi, Republic Day. Designed to display the majesty of the Raj, the grand avenues echo to the sounds of an Independent India.

Such a building is a natural pool of statistics: covering four and a half acres, it encloses twelve separate courtyards in three million cubic feet of stone; it contains three state drawing rooms and a dining room 100ft long. Rumours persist of families of squatters who lived for generations in the more obscure recesses of the house, and of viceregal children who would bicycle between the nursery and the school room. The Viceroy's House was equipped more like a hotel than a home, with its own printing press, laundry, bakery and tailors. It is now the home of the President of India, and although after Partition the building was regarded as the last redoubt of Imperialism, it has stood the test of time and gained the affections of the nation it was built to oppress.

Herbert Baker, left with the task of flanking this marvel with his Secretariats, produced a pair of buildings in a more conventionally Imperial style, although the red and yellow sandstone structures hint playfully at Orientalism. They are almost as highly regarded as the Viceroy's House, as long as attention is distracted from the Orwellian inscription:

LIBERTY WILL NOT DESCEND TO A PEOPLE,
A PEOPLE MUST RAISE THEMSELVES TO LIBERTY,
IT IS A BLESSING WHICH MUST BE EARNED
BEFORE IT CAN BE ENJOYED.

New Delhi was built for the governors, not the governed, and its cool, shady residential streets with their elegant white bungalows in well-watered gardens conceal a nice sense of hierarchy. The designs recognised sixty-one levels of status, and the experienced eye could tell from the size of the portico or layout of the veranda the likely position of the occupant – if the address had not already given the game away. The native princes had their enclave of palaces, too, built with a sense of protocol as rigidly defined as the tables of precedence which determined the number of guns that should salute their arrival at Durbar. New Delhi's domestic architecture concealed an iron bureaucratic fist beneath pretty porches and bougainvillaea, and it is possible to feel something rather sinister and oppressive in its relentlessly leafy loveliness. However, as with all spacious suburban areas, the gardens of New Delhi have caught the property developer's eye, and the battle is now joined to determine whether the bungalow can survive the onslaught of the apartment block.

RIGHT **New Delhi, the Rashtrapati Bhavan. The Moghul/Buddhist/English rose garden.**

Language

Empires wax and wane, but their languages outlive all their other monuments. Latin remained the language of Church, intellectual life and diplomacy for most of the western world until the Reformation, a thousand years after the Sack of Rome. The Turkish that William Hawkins spoke at the Moghul court of Jehangir was understood because that was the language of its forbear, the Mongol Empire. English remains the world's most spoken language long after the sun has set on the British Empire. Language, the stuff of human interaction, is passed on from generation to generation, accreting through use, new meanings and forms, and losing others. Only in literature does language take on material form, able to be stored, researched and retrieved; and only the literature of a language can be stolen, looted or destroyed. Language and literature are the rearguard of Empire, an assimilated relic hard to shake off and full of potent symbols in the minds of formerly subject populations. The English spoken and written in India today often has a vitality and resonance which is at once deeply familiar and wonderfully alien.

Much has been written about the apparent ability of the subcontinent's inhabitants to absorb the successive waves of invaders who have washed over the land. It is possible today to see what is effectively a rural Indian village, complete with tents, cows, fires and pots and pans, on the pavement propped against the imposing British-built flanks of Bombay's central post office, and there is an eerie, but reassuring sense that the tents, fires and cows will be there long after

LEFT The Law Courts, Calcutta. Chaucer and Shakespeare gaze down on unfamiliar surroundings, though both had a keen appreciation of crowds.

RIGHT The National Library, formerly Belvedere House, Calcutta.

LEFT The main Post Office, Bombay.

OPPOSITE Thomas Babington Macaulay, architect of the Indian Penal Code and Raj utilitarian par excellence.

the post office has fallen into abject ruin. There is a similar sense that whilst the Indians had the English language imposed on them, they will overthrow it not by an act of violence but through an almost imperceptible process of absorption.

The proliferation of Indian languages – there are still fourteen official languages and 1,652 designated 'mother tongues' – represented a unique challenge to the servants of the Company in the early days, and one of the principal aims of a Company education, such as that available at the College of Fort William in Calcutta, was to provide a good linguistic grounding: ' . . . I would lead your attention to three branches of study; viz. a scientific and grammatical knowledge of the eastern languages that I would class thus as to utility, Arabic, Persian, Hindoostanee, Sanscrit, Bengalee etc. A personal intercourse with natives of all denominations and castes, to acquire idiom, dialect, manner, local knowledge, knowledge of custom, character, prejudice, religion, internal arrangement, ancient hereditary habits, and distinguishing characteristics. A constant conversation and intercourse with . . . those who are remarkable as classical oriental scholars'. (William Fraser to his younger brother Alexander). Scholarship in the various languages had a highly practical value, and not just in facilitating trade; as Sir William Jones, a Supreme Court Judge, pointed out with justifiable pride, 'I can now read . . . Sanskrit . . . with so much ease that native lawyers can never impose upon the courts in which I sit.' In 1783 Sir William had declared an ambition 'to know India better than any other European ever knew it,' and founded the Asiatic Society in 1784. He benefited from the more enquiring cultural climate that prevailed under the Governor-Generalship of Warren Hastings, succeeding the rapacious era of Clive. The English, having seized Bengal, then wished to examine the trophy more closely: Hastings had encouraged Charles Wilkins to become the first Englishman to master Sanskrit, and he went on to translate the *Bhagavad-gita*.

In this context, Thomas Babington Macaulay's infamous observation that 'a single shelf of a good European library was worth the whole native literature of India and Arabia' can be shown to be that heady mix of energetic ignorance and applied prejudice which characterised the later years of evangelism and utilitarianism in India. Language, as far as he was concerned, was the vehicle for good government and good law. Macaulay was on the Supreme Council in Calcutta from 1834 for a whirlwind four years. He produced the monumental Indian Penal Code (although it was not finally incorporated into law for another twenty years) which was described by Stephen as 'the criminal law of England freed from all technicalities and superfluities, and systematically arranged', requiring only 'a common use of memory and attention' to be understood. It remains a 'founding document of Indian Law'. Utilitarianism, evidently had its uses, but sentiment had no place, as Macaulay's own approving description of his future brother-in-law Charles Trevelyan illustrates: 'He has no small talk. His mind is full of schemes of moral and political improvement . . . his topics, even in courtship, are steam navigation, the education of the natives, the equalisation of the sugar duties'. It was on the foundations of such unswerving practicality that the Raj was built.

Missionaries had established that the cause of the Anglican religion would be best served by education and literacy. This meshed neatly with Macaulay's views that Indians should learn about western thought and science. Being in a position to act, he made English the official language of the Raj Government in 1835, and he made the teaching of English compulsory in the civil service schools that the Government was busy setting up. His aim was to create a westernised, educated 'class of persons, Indian in blood and colour, but English in taste, in opinions, in morals, and in intellect' who could act as 'interpreters between us and the millions'. At the same time he ensured that the law forbidding Indians from high office was substantially relaxed, and thus created the possibility of the newly Anglicised class of persons finding gainful employment within the administration, effectively setting up Indians to rule Indians. This was a very far-sighted policy in many ways; as we have seen, it was the educated Indians who made the first moves towards Indian Nationalism. The English language was thus an instrument of Imperialist oppression in the sense that it tightened controls through the law, the Government and religion. But in so doing it created the possibility of liberation through a newly-educated class who could not only participate in the administration, but had a language in which so to do that was understood throughout the entire country. De Gaulle once famously said of France, 'How can you govern a country that has more than three hundred kinds of cheese?'. Compared to France, India was a positive embarrassment of cheeses (castes, subcastes, tribes, religions, sects, cults, ethnic groups, kingdoms, princely states, languages, dialects . . . to name but a few) before Imperialism welded it together.

BELOW A traffic policeman enforces the law, Bangalore.

The English language was a vital component in the Imperial process. The history of the Tagore family of Bengal reveals the interchange over a long period of English and Indian commercial, cultural, political and religious life. This is particularly evident through the family's most distinguished member, Rabindranath Tagore. He was grandson of Dwarkanath Tagore, an industrialist who helped to found many institutions in Calcutta including the National Library, Calcutta Medical College, the Hindu College and others which were dedicated to the western education of Hindu youth. Rabindranath was destined to become one of the towering figures in Indian history, called by Gandhi 'The Great Sentinel'. Philosopher, poet, songwriter, musician, playwright, educationalist and essayist, he was a man of extraordinary significance to the emergence of a modern Indian cultural identity, but it is his relationship to the English language that concerns us here.

LEFT The full majesty of the Law Courts, Bangalore.

RIGHT A bust of Bengali poet Rabindranath Tagore outside Rabindra Bharati University, Calcutta.

Progressive educational ideas had led to an acceptance of the importance of the teaching of English; Rabindranath, born in 1861 near Calcutta, was a beneficiary of this. It is startling to realise that it was his early exposure to English literature that inspired his intense creativity in Bengali, a language whose literature at the beginning of the nineteenth century was confined to orthodox religious verses in a strictly defined metre. Although he had predecessors in the enrichment of Bengali literature, Tagore's work covers virtually every literary genre. With little to inspire in his own language, he had translated *Macbeth* by the age of twelve, and later Shelley, Rosetti, Swinburne, Hood and Moore – and more. Armed with an English literary tradition, he set about creating a Bengali one which is still revered in India.

He wrote only one poem in English, 'The Child', but his own translations of his songs in *gitanjali* were to create immense interest in England. Written mainly on a voyage to England, when he arrived Tagore showed them to his friend, the painter William Rothenstein, who in turn showed them to Yeats. London's literary lions suddenly had a Bengali tiger amongst them; on 7 July 1912 in Rothenstein's Hampstead drawing room, Yeats read Tagore's poems to an assembly that included Ezra Pound and Alice Meynell. Suddenly, and spectacularly, Tagore's writings in English found an audience, so much so that he was awarded the Nobel Prize for literature in 1913, and a knighthood two years later. Ironically, his star was to fall with almost equal rapidity; his essay on Nationalism in 1916 was badly received in England and the USA, then embroiled in the Great War, and he returned his knighthood after the Massacre of Amritsar. Although a friend of Gandhi, his involvement in the politics of the Independence movement was more inspirational than active. He composed songs for the Bengal Partition protests, meetings of the Indian Congress and even sang from *gitanjali* to Gandhi in jail.

The literary tradition of Indian writers educated and writing in English is large, and continually expanding. In giving Indians a foreign language to write in, the educational policies of the Raj did not just enhance the possibility of their worldwide acceptability and renown; it gave them access to the immense wealth of the English literary tradition, one which – as happened with Tagore in Bengal – was frequently richer than their own – or at least their own contemporary literature. That is not to undermine the enormous influence of the ancient Indian literary tradition, which pervades the religious and cultural heritage of the land: the beauty and power of the Vedic texts – the oldest devotional literature in the world – is undeniable. However, they were written in early Sanskrit, a language that had long ceased to be the vernacular anywhere in India. The great potency of this ancient literature is shown by the reception, which was at times bordering on the hysterical, of the TV series, produced ironically, by an Englishman, Peter Brooke, and based on the later epic, the *Mahabharata*. Meetings in Parliament had to be delayed to fit in with the timing of the show.

ABOVE English is still the language of aspiration.

At the risk of the obvious generalisation, the common feature of Indian writing in English, and it is perhaps inevitable, appears to be an ease with handling spiritual issues. English writers tend to treat Spiritual Issues as something outside of ordinary life, rather than intrinsic to it. Indian writers generally treat death, love, hate, devotion, family and friendship in a way that is suffused with an understated – and frequently unstated – spirituality. The source of this lies again in that fundamental literary tradition of India, the enormously rich and varied Vedic and, later, Sanskrit texts. This wealth of ancient material – the first poem, the *Rigveda-sanhita*, was composed around 1200 BC – was predominantly part of an oral tradition, and the holy texts of the Vedas and *Bhagavad-gita* are still only holy in recitation: the Christian and Muslim veneration of the physical presence of their Holy Books is not part of the Hindu tradition. The written word is less important than the spoken word, and the earliest *Rigveda-sanhita* exemplifies the equivocal, questioning character which could be said to colour the spiritual aspects of contemporary Indian writers in English.

> There was neither the non-existent nor the existent then:
> there was neither the air nor the sky which is beyond it.
> What stirred? Where? In whose protection?
> Was there water, unfathomably deep?
>
> Who truly knows, who will here proclaim
> whence it was produced, whence is this creation?
> The gods came later, with the creation of this universe;
> so who knows whence it has come into being?
>
> *Rigveda-sanhita* 10.129.1, 6-7

The absence of a didactic, preceptive stance is startling; the philosophical arguments appear to grapple with the very genesis of *Genesis*, and it is clear that the comprehension of spiritual issues is more subtle and evolved than in its Biblical counterpart. In this context, it is interesting to note how two later writers responded to the Taj Mahal: 'The ivory gate through which all dreams pass' wrote Kipling; 'a tear on the face of eternity' wrote Tagore. The lyricism of the Englishman is surpassed by the lucidity of the Bengali.

Although its use as a spoken language died out by the third century BC, Sanskrit remained the language of literature, reaching its height in the works of Kalidasa in the fifth century AD. It was only with the arrival of the Muslim invader, Mohammed of Ghazni, at the turn of the millennium that Persian started to become the lingua franca of most of India: like English,

Persian, in its local version of Indo-Persian, was a language imposed by a colonising culture, rich both in its antecedents and contemporary works. As the English were likewise later to do with the Vedas and other ancient texts, the Moghul Akbar commissioned translations from Sanskrit to Persian, which led to the dissemination of Hindu scriptures into Muslim educated circles. It is thus through the twin strands of Sanskrit and Persian that the predominantly oral literary tradition of ancient India became a central feature of the subcontinental culture which was to acquire a new overlay through the English language.

The genre, if that it be, of Indians writing in English is further complicated by those Indians whose upbringing was the result of the other permutations of Empire: indentured labourers from India found their way to other corners of the English globe, like Fiji or the Caribbean. The English literary heritage was taught to their children, such as V. S. Naipaul in Trinidad, in more or less the same way as it would have been in India, with the result that their use of the language is likewise imbued with an indefinable uniqueness. In his first novel, the *Mystic Masseur*, Naipaul perfectly captures the English speech patterns of the Afro-Trinidadians: however, discussion of the effect of an English literary heritage on the rendering of Afro-West Indian English dialogue by an Indian West Indian writing in English lies outside the scope of this work, as we should all be relieved to hear.

BELOW Roy's writing exhibits a powerful love-hate relationship with the English language, which she resents as cultural Imperialism and abuses to frequently sublime effect.

Finally there is the distinguished list of English writers who have attempted to interpret the experience of the British in India, including the unfashionable and misinterpreted Rudyard Kipling, as well as E. M. Forster, John Masters, Paul Scott and Rumer Godden. Predominantly, however, the English were masters of the *Boy's Own* adventures of *My Life on the Frontier* style: confronted with a life so extraordinary, there was no need for recourse to fiction. It is no coincidence that one of the richest fictional works about India, *The Siege of Krishnapur* by J. G. Farrell, draws heavily on contemporary letters and accounts concerning the Mutiny, without the endorsement of which much of the content would scarcely be believable. Likewise the best of George MacDonald Fraser's *Flashman* series are set in the India of the 1840s and 1850s, where Fraser once served: the hero's vast armoury of despicable traits provides a welcome counterpoint to our preconceptions of the stalwart Sahib, and the historical background is always meticulously researched. His *Flashman and the Great Game* contains a particularly horrifying description of the behaviour of European irregular troops roaming the countryside during the Mutiny amusing themselves by slowly hanging any mutineer, or indeed Indian, that they could lay hands on, and watching the 'Pandy's Hornpipe' as they twitched upon the rope. The historical record is noticeably coy when it comes to such matters: the standard histories of the Mutiny tend to be English, and in history, as in all things, 'to the victor, the spoils'.

EDUCATION

It is not surprising that when the English got around to building schools in India, they followed the public school model from which most of them had sprung. Initially, these were for the sons of the English only; gradually scions of the Princely States and higher-ranking Indian officials joined them. After Partition they became the haunt of Anglo-Indians and the sons of the educated, and frequently political, elite. Now they are a strange anachronism, teaching an outmoded English curriculum to a largely uninterested hotchpotch of pupils. With the rise of political gangsterism and decline of the Anglo-Indian, the association between an English education and the ruling elite is no longer automatic, and it is no longer clear exactly what purpose the schools serve. It is ironic that, because the history curriculum in the UK itself now focuses almost exclusively on the twentieth century, Indian school children are far more likely to understand the classic humour of books like *1066 and All That.*

LEFT Schoolboys on the Mall, Darjeeling.

RIGHT Another cricket match in progress, St Paul's School, Darjeeling.

Amongst the most famous of such schools were those founded by Sir Henry Lawrence, Resident at Lahore and erstwhile leader of the Siege of Lucknow. In 1847 the first to be built was at Sanawar, on a hill top near Kasauli donated to him by the Maharajah of Patiala. The ubiquitous Major Hodson of Hodson's Horse supervised the construction, and is remembered by having a particularly taxing cross-country run named after him. His execution by his own hand of the sons of the King of Delhi has apparently given rise to no tide of political correctness at the school, which is perhaps indicative of the colonial bubble in which they survive; such an association would not be permitted in urban India, or even England. Likewise the houses – Roberts, Havelock, Edwardes and Nicholson – are named after the English soldiers we have met in these pages. Lawrence was principally concerned for the education of soldiers' children, who had a tough time on the sweltering Indian plains. The school chapel has been described as 'the most English of all chapels in India'. The school was originally known as the Lawrence Asylum, subsequently the Lawrence Royal Military School, and now the Lawrence School. The 600 pupils (for it has now gone co-educational) sit Cambridge exams, and the school's cricketing prestige is *sans pareil.* Annual dinners for alumni are still held in London. Lawrence College, in the hills near Murree in Pakistan, still flourishes, being the pre-eminent public school in that country. There exists a supranational affinity between the alumni of the Lawrence schools in Pakistan and India, suggesting that the common cultural links forged by their English education outweigh the post-Partition animosity. Another Lawrence foundation at Mount Abu in Rajastan has been converted into a police academy, and a school founded in his honour after his death in the Mutiny at Ootacamund survives under the name of Lovedale. Lawrence died from wounds received on the first day of the Siege of Lucknow, and was buried in the Residency gardens.

OPPOSITE AND LEFT Delhi. Khoonidarwaw, the 'Bloody Gateway'. Under this arch the Moghul Empire brutally ended by the capture of the last Emperor, Bahadur Shah, and the slaying of his two sons by William Hodson after the siege of Delhi in 1857.

ABOVE La Martiniere School, Lucknow. The unlikely legacy of a French adventurer.

Meanwhile in Lucknow itself there is another school which rivals Sanawar for the title of best in India. La Martiniere has a somewhat unusual provenance. It was built in 1781 by Major General Claude Martin to be his home. He was a Lyonnaise who served with distinction in the Company's forces and was later appointed Superintendent of the Arsenal by the Nawab of Lucknow. In this role he amassed sufficient fortune to support his taste in oriental manuscripts and seven Indian mistresses – the latter despite having contracted a virulent form of venereal disease which he was never able entirely to cure. His palace, Farhat Baksh, which now houses La Martiniere school, is an eclectic mix of European, Hindu and Moghul influences, incorporating a drawbridge, two underground floors resembling the 'tykhana' favoured by the Moghuls in hot weather, and a rooftop observatory which contained a telescope signed by William Herschel. In the palace Martin installed his huge library, Boulton and Watt steam engines from Birmingham, an Indian-made replica of Montgolfier's balloon and a collection of sculptures, artefacts and curios, including the plaster handprint of an Irish giant and 'an impaled monkey'. His court included slaves, a French pyrotechnician and a female transvestite masquerading as a eunuch by the name of Myan Jawar. After he failed to negotiate the house's sale to the Nawab, Martin feared it might be seized upon his death and provided in his will that he be buried in an impenetrable vault in the basement, ensuring that it would not be taken over as a result of a Muslim superstition that prevents living over, or disturbing a tomb. When he died in 1800 his vast fortune of over £100,000 was put into a trust which founded, and still finances the school on the site, as well as others in Calcutta and in his home town, Lyons.

From this colourful background sprang a school which was a byword for a pukka British education for scions of the high Raj and later, post-Partition political dynasts. But in the same way as the Anglo-Indians have emigrated as their *raison d'etre* has evaporated, an English education is becoming increasingly anachronistic in an Uttar Pradesh where politics is dominated, not by an educated elite, but by corrupt and venal elements, and a criminal record appears to be a qualification of great value in seeking election to the State Assembly. The English-style public school is likely to wither away the further India moves from its Raj inheritance.

BELOW The Alfred School.

ANGLO-INDIANS

The relaxed moral climate of the East India Company Raj had led to the growth of a significant community of mixed-blood Christian Anglo-Indians who fell between the twin stools of the racial prejudice of the English, the community of their fathers, and the caste prejudice of the Indians, the community of their mothers. Strangely, for a nation much addicted to a particularly hard-line Jesuitical Catholicism, the Portuguese in their enclave in Goa, as well as in their later Brazilian colony, had a much more liberal and welcoming attitude towards their miscegenetic progeny than the British ever showed. Whilst in the late eighteenth century the sons of such unions might be sent to England for schooling – Harrow was a particular favourite – by the nineteenth, attitudes had hardened. In danger of being universal pariahs, the Anglo-Indians' salvation came with Dalhousie's identification of 'the three great engines of social improvement', for it was the Anglo-Indians who neatly co-opted unto themselves the running of the railways, the post and the telegraph, and for a while created very successful communities tied together by pride in a skilled, modern profession. In manner, custom, diet, education and speech resolutely British – but never integrated with them – the Anglo-Indians provided a valuable and loyal interface between the rulers and the ruled in other mid-status roles in administration, the police and customs. Given the British predilection for government at a distance, particularly after the establishment of the hill stations as summer retreats, they depended on good communications for their rule. Anglo-Indians might have been specifically bred for this function, and their role in keeping the telegraph in operation during the Mutiny is regarded by some as pivotal. The mutineers failed to appreciate the strategic value of the telegraph, leaving the lines largely uncut, and enabling vital information about troop movements and outbreaks of insurrection to be relayed around north India. Anglo-Indian communities could be found in all centres of administration and communication, large and small, although the Presidencies attracted the lion's share, and gave them local nicknames: Anglo-Indians from Bombay were known as 'ducks', and those from Madras as 'mulls'.

In the aftermath of the Mutiny, racial theories started to find favour which led to the further stratification of society in India. Anglo-Indians, though valued in second-tier roles, were deemed 'weak' and 'excitable', particularly the womenfolk, whose physical attractions caused the twitch of many a sahib's moustache. During the 1930s, when the writing was already on the wall for the beleaguered community, there was an unsuccessful attempt to establish a homeland for them. McCluskieganj a small town near Ranchi in Bihar was the brainchild of E. T. McCluskie, a businessman and member of the Bengal Legislative Council, apparently inspired by an angelic vision. The Anglo-Indians remained staunchly pro-British in the run-up to Independence, and as late as 1934 they were being taught a song in schools, based on the tune of 'A Bicycle made for Two':

Gandhi, Gandhi,
The cops are after you,
And when they catch you,
You know what they will do –
They'll tie you up with wire
And put you in the black burrow.

Not surprisingly, rejected by the native community, and thus unhealthily dependent on the British, they found themselves in a particularly vulnerable position after Partition; the employment opportunities formerly reserved for them became fair game for all Indians, and many emigrated, principally to Australia, but also to Canada and Britain. They achieved recognition of sorts in the new Constitution of India of 1949: 'an Anglo-Indian means a person whose father or any of whose other male progenitors in the male line is or was of European descent but who is domiciled within the territory of India and is or was born within such territory of parents habitually resident therein and not established there for temporary purposes only . . . ' The perpetuation of the idea that a memsahib would never take up with an Indian is revealing.

ABOVE From the wrong side of the tracks: Ava Gardner smoulders dutifully as the sahib's Anglo-Indian ideal.

The estimated Anglo-Indian population of 200,000 in 1945 fell to 30,000 in 1990, and in India itself gradually dispersed far beyond their original urban communities. At Dumka in Bihar where there was once a thriving community of seventy Anglo-Indians, now just a brother and sister, William and Mary, remain. The schools where they were taught, and the segregated graveyards in which their forebears were buried, have all been quietly absorbed by the Indians. Their children have adopted Hindi names and manners, but still experience prejudice in the job market. The Anglo-Indian is the last living remnant of the Raj, but is likely to disappear in all but purely genetic terms within the next decade. Despite their one-time importance to the British, they rarely feature significantly in any history of the Raj, usually warranting only a passing mention as the community that spawned Englebert Humperdinck and Cliff Richard and a number of useful hockey teams. In India, they are likewise something of an embarrassment, standing accused of being 'trained parrots', aping the British whilst denied the embrace of India's characteristic heterogeneity. At the Grant Govan Homes, a trust-run community for aging Anglo-Indians in Delhi, there are eight cottages, the communal one sporting pictures of the Queen and Prime Minister, and tree planted by the wife of the High Commissioner to commemorate a distant, British, event. Amidst its neatly trimmed lawns and whitewashed walls, the Anglo-Indian will pass into history, the symbiosis with which, by making themselves useful, they were tolerated on the great body of the British Raj, broken by the death of their host.

Epilogue: Whose Raj Was It Anyway?

The Raj in India, from the time of the East India Company to that of the Crown, was disproportionately dominated by non-English colonial subjects of the English Crown in the British Isles, meaning the Irish and the Scots (the Welsh, seemingly less adventurous, did not feature prominently in India). The Duke of Wellington, an Irishman; the Scot, John Mowbray, merchant of Calcutta; General John Nicholson, the Ulsterman and hero of the Siege of Delhi; and the innumerable rank and file of Irish and Scots soldiers in the service of the Company and later the Crown. The history of the British in India shows the extent to which the impoverished sons of the oppressed colonies saw in their Eastern counterpart the opportunity to restore their fortunes; a case of the colonised turned coloniser, it could be said. Until the late nineteenth century, a career in India was considered beneath the sons of aristocratic English families and, if a noble scion was spotted in India, it was probably through the necessity of fleeing some financial indiscretion. Whilst a significant contribution to the fortunes of Britain were made by the Irish and the Scots, the English stayed at home to enjoy the consequences.

Yet it is the image of the Englishman which is retained in empire mythology, the pukka sahib with the stiff upper lip and a firm but fair hand with the natives. Perhaps 'Englishman' is simply a flag of convenience because the word 'Britisher' is so unwieldy. However, there would seem to be more to it than that, as this cartoon image cannot readily be switched to an Irishman or a Scot: the clothes simply don't fit. It would seem that having effectively sent the less fortunate of their fellow island inhabitants off to do their dirty work for them, the English not only appropriated the lion's share of the spoils, but airbrushed the collective colonial memory so that only the image of the Englishman remained. And where can we find that Englishman now? Whereas the Scots and the Irish have retained a strong sense of national identity, the loss of the Empire has exposed the conjuring trick, and the English stand revealed as illusionists at the last. Building an empire, as we have seen, is as much a matter of self-belief as anything, and when that belief is lost, identity evaporates like a will-o'-the-wisp.

The fact that the English themselves have had no coherent national identity to fall back on is no surprise; racially and culturally a mongrel nation at best, they defined themselves initially by the narrow confines of their island home, but later on the playing fields of Empire. When Cecil Rhodes said that to have been born English was to have won first prize in the lottery of life, could that have been because the English had been clever enough to persuade the Irish and Scots to do their bidding? Could Mr. Banks in 'Mary Poppins' have ever sung 'It nice to be a Irishman in 1910, King Edward's on the throne, Its the Age of Men'?

It is an historical curiosity that a country that had a highly evolved domestic political system which defended the individual's rights against state oppression should be such successful Imperialists, the ruling ethos of which is a de facto assertion of the rights of the state over its subject peoples. It is as if the free-born Englishman naturally assumed that even his rule would be beneficent because he was a product of a such a country. And, by comparison, he was right: the much-maligned British Empire was appreciably 'better' than those of its contemporary European counterparts: better run, less corrupt, less cruel, more just, more enlightened. The fact that it fell short of the Arcadia that revisionists have attempted to compare it with is more a reflection of our times than those of our Imperial forbears.

ABOVE Like their counterparts in England, the bandstands of India echo to the long-departed strains of 'Rule Britannia'. Eden Gardens, Calcutta.

One result of the success of the Raj was that Britain, naturally insulated from Europe by geography, could turn its back on the troubled affairs of its continental neighbours. In 1866 Disraeli cheerfully referred to the country as 'really more than an Asiatic power than a European', and this attitude was echoed by both sides in the Second World War: Hitler would have been quite prepared to treat with Britain on the basis that he would rule Europe and she could maintain her eastern Empire. Likewise, serious consideration was given to the idea of moving the Government of Britain to India. It was a delusion of course, as India itself was showing all the turbulent symptoms of its coming Independence, but the English had successfully peddled delusions to the subcontinent before, sustaining its control of 250 million people through a European presence that never exceeded 125,000. The idea of a Britain independent of European concerns has had lasting political consequences into our time. The unhealthy imbalance in the country's relationship with the United States is one; the knee-jerk resistance to pan-European politics is another.

Britain's relationship to India, and particularly as we have seen, England's, runs more deeply than that of master and servant. The particular affection that the English population – generally the more elderly and educated – have for the Raj is compounded by nostalgia for a lost sense of their own identity. It is not just that the English mourn the loss of their Imperial status, and the power and the glory that went with it. In a very real sense the English were never closer to the English of their own myths than they were in India – never more courageous than when facing down the Afghan jezails, never more stoical than when besieged by Mutineers, never more magnanimous to defeated enemies, never more charitable to the poor and oppressed, never more just, more sporting, more God-fearing, more reasonable, more dynamic. India provided a grand stage for the exhibition of the character traits that the British most admired in themselves, a fabulous backdrop and an exotic chorus of teeming millions to play off. After the curtain fell, and the applause faded, they became a much diminished, ordinary people.

Index